Shadowland

Wales 3000–1500 BC

Shadowland

Wales 3000–1500 BC

Steve Burrow

AMGUEDDFA CYMRU –
NATIONAL MUSEUM WALES

OXBOW BOOKS
Oxford & Oakville

Co-published by
Oxbow Books and Amgueddfa Cymru – National Museum Wales

© Oxbow Books, The National Museum of Wales and Steve Burrow 2011

ISBN 978-1-84217-459-3

This book is available direct from

Oxbow Books, Oxford, UK
(Phone: 01865-241249; Fax: 01865-794449)

and

The David Brown Book Company
PO Box 511, Oakville, CT 06779, USA
(Phone: 860-945-9329; Fax: 860-945-9468)

or from our website

www.oxbowbooks.com

A CIP record for this book is available from the British Library

Library of Congress Cataloging-in-Publication Data

Burrow, Steve.
  Shadowland : Wales 3000-1500 BC / Steve Burrow.
    p. cm.
  Includes index.
  ISBN 978-1-84217-459-3
  1. Prehistoric peoples--Wales. 2. Megalithic monuments--Wales. 3. Tools,
Prehistoric--Wales. 4. Quarries and quarrying, Prehistoric--Wales. 5. Wales--Antiquities.
I. National Museum of Wales. II. Title.
  GN806.W3B87 2011
  936.2'9--dc23
                        2011033537

Printed in Wales by
Gomer Press, Llandysul, Ceredigion

Contents

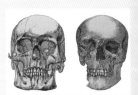

Acknowledgements

My exploration of the period covered by this book has been made much easier by the help of colleagues who have made freely available the results of their own work and who have been generous in their criticism of mine. It has also benefited from the support of many curators at other museums who have opened their doors and facilitated my study of their collections. I have done my best to acknowledge them all below, and apologise sincerely to any I have unwittingly left out.

Martin Green, Peter Harp, David Jenkins, Frances Lynch, Chris Musson, Stuart Needham, Fiona Roe, Dave Weddle and John Ll Williams. Dave and Sue Chapman (Ancient Arts), Esther Roberts (Bangor Museum), Peredur Lynch (Bangor University), Richard Cuttler and Ann Woodward (Birmingham Archaeology), Tim Darvill (Bournemouth University), Alex Gibson (Bradford University), Edmund Parsons (Brenig Visitor Centre), George Nash (Bristol University), Ben Roberts and Gillian Varndell (British Museum), Jonathon Berry, Gwilym Hughes and Sian Rees (Cadw), Simon Timberlake (Cambridge Archaeological Unit), Tom Jones (Cardiff Archaeological Society), Jacqui Mulville and Alasdair Whittle (Cardiff University), Gavin Evans (Carmarthen Museum), Jenny Britnell, Ian Grant, Nigel Jones and Chris Martin (Clwyd-Powys Archaeological Trust), Deborah Snow (Flintshire Museum Service), Sian James and Edric Roberts (Great Orme Ancient Copper Mines), Andrew Davidson, Jane Kenney, David Longley and George Smith (Gwynedd Archaeological Trust), Keith Ray (Herefordshire County Council), Astrid Caseldine (Lampeter University), Corina Westwood (Museum of Island History), Alison Sheridan (National Museums Scotland), Peter Northover and Rick Schulting (Oxford University), Eva Bredsdorf (Powysland Museum), Toby Driver and Tom Pert (Royal Commission on the Ancient and Historical Monuments of Wales), Tom Booth and Andrew Chamberlain (Sheffield University), Peter Boyd and Cameron Moffett (Shrewsbury Museum & Art Gallery), John Griffith Roberts (Snowdonia National Park), Mark Lewis (Tenby Museum), Tim Mighall (University of Aberdeen), Gabriel Cooney and Muiris O'Sullivan (University College Dublin), Julie Gardiner, Tom Goskar and Jacqueline McKinley (Wessex Archaeology), Jonathon Gammond (Wrexham County Borough Museum). Also my colleagues at Amgueddfa Cymru – National Museum Wales: Edward Besly, Richard Bevins, Ken Brassil, Richard Brewer, Shanon Burrow, Jackie Chadwick, Evan Chapman, Tom Cottrell, Tony Daly, Mary Davis, Jody Deacon, Angela Gaffney, Adam Gwilt, Ashley McAvoy, Louise Mumford, Mark Redknap, Julie Taylor, Kevin Thomas, Elizabeth Walker and Sian Williams.

Some of the research relied on in this book was carried out with the generous support of grants from Cadw, the Friends of Amgueddfa Cymru – National Museum Wales and the Oxford Radiocarbon Accelerator Dating Service.

The original illustrations have been produced by Jackie Chadwick and Tony Daly, and many of the studio photographs were taken by Kevin Thomas and James Wild. Astrid Caseldine, Tom Cottrell, Tim Darvill, Alex Gibson, Sian James, Alison Sheridan, Simon Timberlake and Ann Woodward read parts of the text, and Edward Besly, Shanon Burrow, Mary Davis, Jody Deacon, Del Elliott, Adam Gwilt, Frances Lynch, Ashley McAvoy, Phil Morgan, Stuart Needham and John Griffiths Roberts read the book in its entirety. All have enhanced its contents and I am very grateful for their suggestions and guidance.

Shadowland is dedicated to my daughter, Caitlin Joy Ida Burrow.

Introduction

The shadows

This is the story of life in Wales over a period of 1,500 years, as gleaned from the remains its inhabitants left behind. These people had no writing, so they have left us no names and no records of their deeds. Instead we have the possessions they treasured in life, the broken remains of their bodies, and the marks they left on the landscape. The people of this time are separated from us by over one hundred and seventy generations, a colossal gulf which archaeologists seek to bridge with tools which shed light across millennia. It is the same project that has been undertaken for all periods in Wales, some far more ancient, but the results in this instance have been remarkable. Sometimes the periods uncovered by archaeologists and explored by historians are easily, if incompletely, grasped by popular imagination: the kingdoms of the Middle Ages, the Empire of Rome, Celtic tribes, megalithic tomb builders, and Neanderthals to name a few. But names have failed to adhere to the people of 3000 to 1500 BC. The best known, 'Beaker people', does not fill many palates with a potent historical flavour. Equally impenetrable are the archaeological classifications which cover this period: Late Neolithic, Chalcolithic, Early Bronze Age. This is of interest in itself; despite two hundred years of archaeological enquiry, the people of these fifteen centuries have remained essentially anonymous, in contrast to those who lived both before and after them. Here then is the shadowland covered by this book.

In part these shadows have fallen by choice: from 3000 to 2200 BC people built few monuments and buried very few of the worldly goods which they must certainly have possessed. In the absence of such time capsules much of the evidence for their lives has reached archaeologists by chance – often when they were looking for other things. But this is not the case for the period 2200 until 1500 BC when monuments were built in profusion and the dead were buried in great numbers. Here the shadows are thick because of problems of interpretation: the lives revealed seem filled with rituals that defy easy comprehension, and the motivations of those who lived them are difficult to grasp. Most perplexing of all is the simple absence of the mundane across all this period. Thousands of burials are known, dozens of meeting places and ceremonial centres have been uncovered, but hardly any settlements or houses. It is as though the people themselves were shadows, who gained substance in times of ritual and mourning.

But despite all this shadow play great works are evident. Around 2600 BC a community living in what is now a sparsely occupied part of central Wales built the largest timber enclosure to have been found anywhere in Britain. Around the same time, in southwest Wales, around eighty stones each weighing about four tonnes, were hauled over 200km to southern England where they now form a part of Stonehenge. These were the works of giants. Around 1700 BC work began carving copper ore from the flanks of the Great Orme on the north Wales coast, in a process which would, hundreds of years later, create the largest mine in Europe. Here, and at other mines in north and west Wales, people who must have seemed like magicians turned this ore into gleaming axe heads and razor-edged daggers. Perhaps most astonishing of all is the transformation of the landscape which had occurred by 1500 BC; by this date in all parts of Wales burial mounds dotted mountains, river valleys, and plains. It was to be many years before another building project was to leave such a decisive mark on the country.

Before 3000 BC

To begin a history 5,000 years ago is to look back deep into the origins of our world, and it would be easy to view the people at the start of this book as pioneers discovering new things in a virgin land, but this was not the case. At 3000 BC, Wales was already an ancient land occupied for millennia. Its peaks and rivers were presumably known by long-fixed names, the best places to farm, fish and hunt had been identified, and the patterns of the country's seasons had become ingrained in the consciousness. The woods which covered much of the land may still have been wild, but the paths which led through them to link river valleys and uplands would have been well known. And just as a modern archaeologist sees traces of former lives in the land around them, so too would these people.

Most ancient were the many thousands of stone tools discarded across the landscape – arrowheads, scrapers and knives of unfamiliar design but familiar purpose. Some of these tool makers had lived and died nine millennia before: fur-wrapped hunters following reindeer and catching fish at the end of the Ice Age. When the climate improved their descendants continued to drop their worn out flints while hunting, fishing and gathering plants in a densely wooded land. These truly early people have left few other traces of their presence – shadows themselves, but shadows of a

Flint tools made almost 13,000 years ago, after Wales emerged from beneath the melting glaciers.
Nanna's Cave (Pembrokeshire).
© The National Museum of Wales (Jim Wild). Original artefacts housed in the collections of Amgueddfa Cymru – National Museum Wales. (Largest example 5.8cm long).

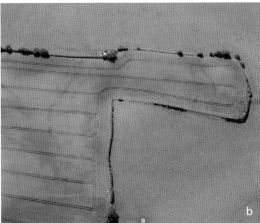

a. A megalithic tomb chamber, probably built to house a community's dead around 3650 BC.
Garn Llwyd (Monmouthshire). © The National Museum of Wales (Steve Burrow).

b. A causewayed enclosure, one of the meeting places of the first farmers. Today the only traces of this site are the filled-in ditch circuits which mark out its circumference. Crops growing in these ditches appear darker than in the rest of the field.
Lower Womaston (central Powys¹). © Crown copyright (Royal Commission on the Ancient and Historical Monuments of Wales).

c. A double-ditched cursus can be seen running across the centre of this image. These monuments date from the years after 3600 BC and are found across Britain. Their purpose remains unknown.
Sarn-y-bryn-caled (northern Powys). © Clwyd-Powys Archaeological Trust.

¹ Throughout this book, modern unitary authority boundaries have been preferred in describing the location of sites, with the exception of those in Powys. This massive authority stretches from the Berwyn Mountains in the north to the Brecon Beacons in the south, and is too broad a descriptor to be of much use to the reader. Instead this area is split into three: northern, central and southern Powys, corresponding broadly with the old counties of Montgomeryshire, Radnorshire and Breconshire respectively. Vale of Glamorgan unitary authority is also abbreviated to Glamorgan.

different kind from the ones who occupy this book. Reliant on nature's providence they seem to have trod lightly, managing rather than controlling their environment and possessing little. When they show themselves to archaeologists it is more often as countryside stewards and rarely as the dark obsessives of death and ritual who were to follow them.

More epic in their proportions were the ruinous remains of stone-framed tombs built by the first farmers around 800 years before this book begins. These had probably been intended to reinforce a claim on the land – and the fact that over a hundred survive today is a testament to the success, albeit partial, of this ambition. But for most people of 3000 BC these were symbols of a different age, still recognisable as tombs, and occasionally used as such, but not a central part of their own culture. Of similar antiquity were the meeting places of the first farmers: these were circles of banks and ditches about 200m across and split by numerous causeways. Pottery made in a long-abandoned style may have been visible in the eroding sides of these monuments along with occasional pieces of bone, some of it human.

Most recent were rectangular earthworks of parallel banks and ditches, around 20m wide and hundreds of metres long which had been dug across Wales. Many of these had only been abandoned a few generations before 3000 BC, and their banks were probably now topped by fresh tree growth with their ditches silting up – a minor obstacle to be crossed or walked around, en route to a destination. Today they are known as cursus monuments, since William Stukeley, who rediscovered them in the eighteenth century, likened them to Roman chariot tracks; but their original function continues to be debated. At 3000 BC their purpose may still have been remembered.

Of all these ancestral traces, the tombs probably continued to exert the strongest pull on the people of 3000 BC, indeed this story really begins with the last substantial gasp of the tomb building cultures in Wales.

Part 1

3000 – 2200 BC

Location of sites in Wales mentioned in this chapter.

1 Abercynafon
2 Barclodiad y Gawres
3 Bryn Celli Ddu
4 Brynderwen
5 Capel Garmon
6 Castell Bryn Gwyn
7 Corntown
8 Daylight Rock
9 Four Crosses
10 Goldcliff
11 Gop
12 Graig Lwyd
13 Gwaenysgor
14 Gwernvale
15 Lavan Sands
16 Llanafan Fawr
17 Llanbedr
18 Llanbedr Dyffryn Clwyd
19 Llanbedrgoch
20 Llandegai
21 Lower Luggy
22 Maesmor
23 Meusydd
24 Nant Helen
25 Ogmore-by-Sea
26 Penmachno
27 Preseli Hills
28 Sarn-y-bryn-caled
29 Sker House
30 Thornwell Farm
31 Trefignath
32 Trelystan
33 Ty-Isaf
34 Upper Ninepence
35 Waun Fignen Felen
36 Ysceifiog

© The National Museum of Wales (Jackie Chadwick, Tony Daly).

The years around 3000 BC

The last of the tomb builders

At some time in the decades around 3000 BC a community marked out a plot of land on Anglesey as the site of their ancestral tomb. It is not known why they picked the location they did – possibly it was because it was close to an enclosure that had been abandoned a few centuries before, less likely they noticed the postholes of a building which had occupied this place some three thousand years earlier.

The planning of the tomb was carefully done. A post was set upright, and then the builders waited for a clear midsummer morning when they could mark out a line to fix the point where the sun rose on the horizon. An arc of standing stones was then positioned around the post to highlight both this alignment and the orientation which the tomb chamber and passage walls would occupy. Fragments of cremated bone were placed beneath some of these standing stones and in pits within the area they defined.

Great slabs of stone were then dragged into position, probably from beside a rock outcrop about 150m away, and the chamber took shape. Then the passage was built, carefully following the lines that had been marked out previously. While work progressed a large slab carved with swirling patterns was dragged to its position behind the chamber and the whole monument was encased in a mound, the earth for which was dug from a ditch which encircled the whole. But the building was not yet finished. Another year passed and the alignment of the passage was checked to ensure that the rising sun would fall on the rear wall of the tomb's chamber. The alignment was a success and a window of light illuminated the chamber as anticipated, but still more could be done to highlight the drama of the effect. Further additions were made to the passage, narrowing and extending it, increasing the precision with which the tomb caught the rising midsummer sun – warming the cremated bones of the community's dead forever.

This tomb which is now known as Bryn Celli Ddu, 'the Mound of the Dark Grove', was excavated in the 1920s by one of Wales's great archaeologists, W J Hemp. So meticulous are his records of his work that it allowed the author to return to his

Above: Bryn Celli Ddu (Anglesey).
© The National Museum of Wales (Steve Burrow).

Right: Sunrise on the midsummer solstice, viewed from the chamber.
© National Museum of Wales (Steve Burrow).

Below: The construction of Bryn Celli Ddu.
The tomb was probably begun as a short monument broadly aligned on the midsummer sunrise,
subsequent enlargement lengthened and narrowed its passage, refining the alignment still further.
Ditch and mound shown as dark and light tones. Stones are marked in black.
© The National Museum of Wales (Tony Daly).

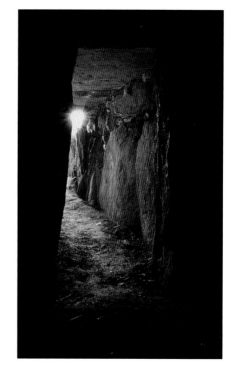

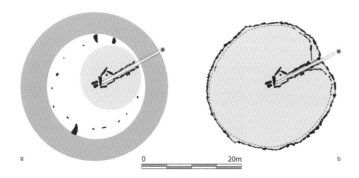

Designs carved on stones at passage tombs on Anglesey. Top, Bryn Celli Ddu; centre and bottom, Barclodiad y Gawres.

© The National Museum of Wales (Tony Daly).

archive almost eighty years later, to study his site notebooks and to radiocarbon date some of the charcoal and human bones which he had carefully preserved. This, in turn, allowed the history of the site to be understood, but the most important development in the story of Wales's last tomb builders has come as a result of excavation at sites in other countries. These have served to identify the builders of Bryn Celli Ddu as adherents of a specific millennia-old burial tradition found along the shores of Atlantic Europe from Portugal to Brittany, and from Ireland to Orkney. The people who adopted this tradition, which probably has its origin in the southern part of this 2,500km long distribution, were united in the construction of round mounds, pierced by passages leading to concealed chambers, hence the name 'passage tombs'.

The passage tomb tradition reached its apogee in the massive tombs of Ireland, some of which were probably built a century or two before Bryn Celli Ddu and which are profusely decorated with swirling and jagged carvings. The carvings at Bryn Celli Ddu are confined to just two stones, but in Wales the finest surviving examples of this art are to be found at Barclodiad y Gawres, 'the Apronful of the Giantess', a cliff-top tomb on the west coast of Anglesey. Excavation began here in 1952, led by Terence Powell of Liverpool University and Glyn Daniel from Cambridge; both were key figures in the study of megalithic tombs and were well-placed to interpret their findings. Their work revealed a passage leading to a central chamber from which opened three side chambers. The capstones of these structures had already been removed, and the contents of the chambers pillaged, but the designs on the wall survived. Powell and Daniel recognised carvings on three stones at the entrance to the main chamber and on the rear wall of two of the side chambers, and since their work George Nash has led a project which has identified one more example. The most dramatic of these carvings takes the form of a stylised figure, positioned at the opening of passage to chamber. The shape of the stone suggests the figure's outline, with the torso picked out with zigzagged lines and chevrons. This figure, and a stone pillar found in the chamber at Bryn Celli Ddu, may have been symbolic guardians of their tombs, their form being based on less abstract examples found in Brittany.

At Barclodiad y Gawres this guardian watches those who enter, while at Bryn Celli Ddu it is set in permanent shadow, always watching for the midsummer sun that lights the rear wall of the chamber from the darkness.

Other examples of this art are known from Wales, for example in Ardudwy, Gwynedd. Here a spiral, characteristic of this style, but present also in later traditions, was found 'on the hills near some early stone remains' and was subsequently set inside the Church of St Peter in Llanbedr in Gwynedd. Presumably there was a tomb of this type in this area, the stone being salvaged from it during its demolition. A similar spiral-carved stone was built into St Afan's Church at Llanafan Fawr in southern Powys, although here specialists believe it may be a product of early medieval hands. Less controversially, in the grounds of Calderstones Park in Liverpool are the remains of another tomb, its badly damaged stones covered in carvings of spirals, zigzags and, curiously, feet. These were the last tombs to be built in this part of Britain, ending an ancient tradition of megalithic construction, and there is little evidence that the ideas of these passage tomb builders spread beyond these coastal regions.

Of the passage tomb builders themselves little remains. They cremated their dead and only small fragments of their bones have survived to the present. Whether they were native people experimenting with a foreign tradition, or settlers from Ireland or even further afield is unknown. But since neither Bryn Celli Ddu or Barclodiad y Gawres seem to have been used for a great length of time after their construction, it is likely that in the centuries that followed, the descendants of these people turned their back on this way of life, adopting instead more widely held cultural norms. It was to be the last time that the people of Wales were to involve themselves in such an international phenomenon for over 500 years. Over this period, innovations were insular and their origins can be found within Britain and Ireland.

Carvings on a stone at The Calderstones (Liverpool).
© George Nash, Adam Stanford.

The mound which tops Gop Hill (Flintshire) is the largest in Wales. It has been argued that it may be a passage tomb, but limited excavation in the nineteenth century failed to locate a chamber. The opening to Gop Cave, a burial place definitely used around 3000 BC, can be seen in the limestone cliff below the mound.

© Crown copyright (Royal Commission on the Ancient and Historical Monuments of Wales).

Old ideas made new

The designs of the passage tomb users were introduced to a country which had largely abandoned tomb building and was looking for new ways to express itself; but occasional hints survive, both in Wales and further afield, to suggest that some elements of their culture had more far reaching influences.

One hint of a cultural legacy from the passage tomb builders of the Irish Sea shores, and indeed from other contemporary burial traditions, comes in the marked preference for circular monuments apparent in the years around 3000 BC.

Around 3100 BC, possibly earlier, a circular enclosure, known today as Llandegai A was built in a clearing near Bangor, just 9km east of Bryn Celli Ddu but separated from it by the Menai Straits. The enclosure consisted of a ditch, dug in a circle over 90m in diameter, the soil from which was piled up in the interior to form a bank which may have been over 3m tall. A comparatively narrow 1.3m wide entrance pierced both bank and ditch.

Within the enclosure, close to the inside of the bank, was a pit in which had been placed bones from a cremation, sealed below a large stone. Also in the pit was a stone used for polishing stone axes, some pottery and fragments of shell. On the other side of the enclosure another pit held a stone axe. Just outside the entrance a smaller roughly circular arrangement of pits was dug, just 9m in diameter, and within these were placed more cremated human remains. Stuart Needham has suggested that these pits may once have held stones or timbers for walls, raising the possibility that they mark the remains of a small building.

It is not known why this large enclosure was built. If it were intended as the boundary of a farmstead one might expect more food and artefact debris. Furthermore, the scale of the construction suggests it was the work of several families – presumably engaged in an enterprise which they felt would benefit them all. Such a commonly held purpose suggests a meeting place in the broadest sense of the term, while the burial of cremated remains inside and outside the enclosure may have served to sanctify the site in a manner which echoes practices at passage tombs. But while tombs were built as houses for the dead, at Llandegai A it seems the dead were no longer segregated in their own world, but were used in the affairs of the living.

Similar evidence can be found at other broadly contemporary enclosures. At Stonehenge a circular enclosure 110m in diameter was dug around 2950 BC, centuries before the erection of the massive stones for which the site is now more famous, and large numbers of cremation burials were placed in the ditch and in pits inside it. A century or two earlier another 100m diameter enclosure had been dug at Flagstones in Dorset. Abstract designs, reminiscent of passage tomb art, but not exactly comparable, were carved into the chalk walls of the ditch, and the dead were lain on its base.

Returning to Wales, further excavated sites which may belong to this tradition include Ysceifiog in Flintshire and Castell Bryn Gwyn on Anglesey. The 100m diameter enclosure at Ysceifiog was dug by Cyril Fox in 1925 as part of his campaigns to date and interpret Offa's Dyke which butts this enclosure. Fox dug two narrow trenches across the ditch with little result, leaving the site essentially undated. But in both size and its determined circularity it is very similar to both Llandegai A and Stonehenge. Furthermore, within the enclosure was a massive grave pit which, it will be argued later, probably dates to this time. Castell Bryn Gwyn is slightly smaller at 77m across but mirrors Llandegai A in having a narrow entrance on the west southwest side. The enclosure entrance was dug by Geoffrey Wainwright in 1959 and 1960 and within a cobbled surface was found a sherd of pottery which can be dated to the centuries around 3000 BC.

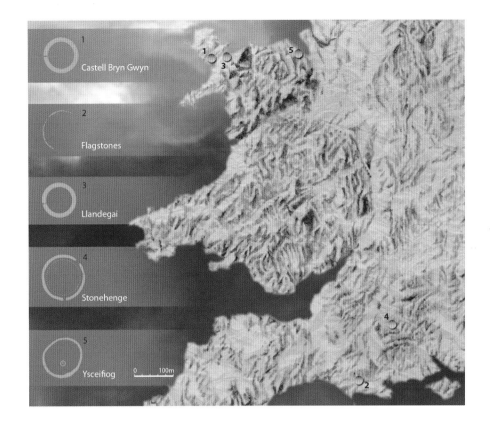

Plans and locations of excavated enclosures which probably date to around 3000 BC.

© The National Museum of Wales (Jackie Chadwick, Tony Daly).

1 Castell Bryn Gwyn

2 Flagstones

3 Llandegai

4 Stonehenge

5 Ysceifiog

0   100m

The dead in the service of the living

The cremated remains in the enclosure at Llandegai A were those of an adult, probably a woman, buried in a skin bag. Over a kilogram of bone was found by the excavators, suggesting that her remains had been gathered from the pyre and buried in their entirety. In the smaller circle of pits outside the entranceway, the picture was more complex. In one were bones from two adults, a newborn infant, and possibly others; in another, fragments from an adult and an infant. The burial of bones from more than one individual is hinted at in some of the other pits, and it seems that between six and sixteen people were interred in total. But the cremated remains only include parts of bodies, sometimes, just a few scraps – like those sealed below the mound at Bryn Celli Ddu. This was not a simple case of burial, but rather the marking of a site using a community's bones.

A similar 'token burial' may have been made in the valley of the River Severn, at Sarn-y-bryn-caled, where a very similar small circle was dug around 2900 BC, albeit with a continuous ditch rather than pit segments. In the base of the ditch, beside the entrance were placed the cremated remains of a young person, possibly a woman. The ditch then silted up, before being cleaned out at which time the remains of three more cremations were placed near the entranceway. After this, the users of the Sarn-y-bryn-caled enclosure had to pass through an entranceway flanked by representatives of the dead. In the case of the youth in the base of the ditch, all parts of the body were present, but not all of their fragmentary bones – probably less than half. It is possible that this was all that could be found in the mess of the funeral pyre, but the decision not to include all of the remains may have been deliberate; indeed two of the later cremations were only represented by very small token quantities of bone.

Ceremony at Sarn-y-bryn-caled (northern Powys).

Around 3000 BC a circular ditch was cleaned out and cremated remains were placed in its base. Was this a community returning to the site of an abandoned house and honouring its former occupants, or the long-lived use of a ceremonial enclosure?

© National Museum of Wales (Tony Daly).

Burial rites

The number of token burials known from this period raises obvious questions about what happened to the rest of these bodies and, equally importantly, what happened to the many other thousands of people who probably died in Wales each year. The burial of a few in north Wales's passage tombs has already been described; elsewhere in Wales the picture is less clear.

The examples given above show that some people were cremated, and to this list can be added an adult woman found cremated in a pit within an enclosure at Lower Luggy in northern Powys, and the placing of the remains of another cremation beside a post in a timber circle at Meusydd, also in northern Powys. But, despite the resilience of burnt bone to the destructive effect of Wales's acid soils, cremated remains from this period are not often found. If the practice was common, the ashes were either not buried deep enough, or were not buried at all, reducing their chances of surviving to the present.

Ring ditch and two timber circles at Meusydd (northern Powys).

The ring ditch, the remains of an Early Bronze Age burial monument, is the dark circular feature in the middle of the photograph. The cremated remains described in the text were found in the small timber circle to its right, while the circle to its left remains undated.

All three monuments were dug by Nigel Jones of Clwyd-Powys Archaeological Trust.

© Cambridge University Collection of Air Photographs.

Some bones still found their way into megalithic tombs, demonstrating that the funerary role which these places had served centuries before was still remembered, despite their outwardly ruinous appearance. For example, at Thornwell Farm in Monmouthshire bodies were interred among ancient bone piles around 3300 and 3000 BC. Perhaps there was comfort to be had in putting the recent dead into such ancient company. Certainly there is nothing to suggest that these tombs were feared by later peoples.

Gop Cave in Flintshire provides another instance where reuse of an ancient burial place can be clearly demonstrated. The cave was explored in the late 1880s by William Boyd Dawkins who records finding a stone-walled enclosure within which were crammed the remains of at least fourteen people. The space was too small for them all to have been buried at once, so the early ones must have rotted to bone before the last were interred. There was also evidence that some of the bones had been ordered, with long bones being stacked together, and some set upright. Boyd Dawkins also found bones scattered outside the chamber. Over a century after his work, a radiocarbon dating programme organised by Rick Schulting of Oxford University has shed light on the duration over which Gop Cave was in use. The first body in the chamber was probably put in around 3650 BC, the heyday of the tomb builders, and the last dated body was added between 3000 and 2900 BC. It is likely that many other ancient burial places were reused at this time since contemporary pottery has been found at several, including Capel Garmon in Conwy and possibly Trefignath on Anglesey; but once newly added bones have acquired the same patina of age as their older companions the only way to tell them apart is to radiocarbon date all individuals in a chamber. This process is expensive, destructive, and rarely undertaken.

The reuse of the Gop Cave 'tomb' and the experimentation with passage tombs and their burial rites might give the impression that all of Wales was backward-looking at this time, toying with the ideas of previous generations, but two sites hint that more novel practices were also current.

Around 3000 BC a pit was dug and two people buried on Long Mountain, a ridge overlooking the valley of the River Severn. The site, known as Trelystan, was excavated by Bill Britnell of the Clwyd-Powys Archaeological Trust, and he reconstructed the scene as follows. A community dug into and prised out the bedrock of the hill until they had made a pit almost 3m long, 1.5m wide and 0.6m deep, with a deeper slot cut in the middle of its base. A wooden coffin long enough to hold an adult was set in the pit and a body placed inside. A container holding the cremated remains of a woman was then either set in the coffin with the inhumation, or was placed beside it. The woman had had a few flints, including a knife, with her when she was cremated, and these accompanied her into the pit. With a lid set on the coffin the pit was filled in and the remaining rock was piled up to make a rough cairn over the top. In time, the coffin rotted away, its shape being preserved by the cairn which slumped into the space above the corpse. The body in the coffin was itself eaten away by the acid soils, bones and all, until only the hard fragments of a few teeth remained.

A very similar burial site of roughly the same date has been found an easy day's walk north of Trelystan on the edge of the floodplain of the River Severn. Here, at Four Crosses, a team led by Walt Warrilow found another pit, at the centre of a 21m diameter encircling ditch. This time the pit was roughly circular with a diameter varying from 3.8 to 4.5m, dug over 1.4m deep into gravel. An adult had been interred in the middle, laid on its left side, with legs crouched and arms pulled against the chest, and a jaw bone, presumed to be from a calf had been placed beside its arms, along with a small pear-shaped piece of stone. Beside this person's head was the

Burial scene at Four Crosses (northern Powys), around 3000 BC.

© National Museum of Wales (Tony Daly).

Pit grave at Ysceifiog (Flintshire), excavated in 1925 by Cyril Fox.

Fox believed that this grave, set within the 100m diameter enclosure described above, was dug between 2000 and 1500 BC, but re-analysis by Chris Musson has highlighted its similarity to the early graves found at Four Crosses and Trelystan.

The picture shows the landowner (left) beside Cyril Fox (right). The landowner had been unwilling to be photographed in the pit, superstitious of the consequences, until Fox offered to bear half the risk.

© National Museum of Wales.

remains of a pottery bowl. Presumably these were offerings from grieving relatives – meat, a talisman, and a bowl which may have held more food or drink. They had not been buried alone. Two small grave-like slots had been cut into the floor of the pit at their head and feet and a crouched body placed in each. A few flints were discarded or lost when the pit was filled in, and some charcoal, probably from an adjacent patch of burning was also incorporated. As at Trelystan the bodies were eaten away by acid soils, their shadowed outlines being preserved this time in blackish-purple by manganese dioxide. Similar graves are known at Ysceifiog, where a large pit held the remains of a man, fringed by a black deposit which may have been the remains of a wooden coffin. And at Meole Brace, near Shrewsbury, where a grave was found encircled by a ditch which was very similar in form to that found at both Four Crosses and Ysceifiog. A radiocarbon date suggested that the monument had been built before 3000 BC, although this is not certain since the charcoal used to date the site might predate the ditch.

The similarity between these burials, all found between the River Dee and the northern arc of the River Severn suggest a common approach to death in this area, albeit with elements of the grave design bearing comparison with sites in other parts of Britain.

But all of these graves seem to have been isolated monuments, not components in large cemeteries suggesting that only a small part of the community was buried in this way. It is possible therefore that these graves represent special events, and to continue this theme it is interesting that at both Trelystan and Four Crosses, the grave contained more than one body. The couple at Trelystan may have died at the same time, although it is possible that the remains of the cremated woman were stored for some time until her burial with the other individual. But at Four Crosses an explanation is needed which accounts for three people dying at almost the same time, since the grave seems only to have been dug and filled once. Further afield, at Monkton Up Wimborne in Dorset, the excavator, Martin Green, has suggested that sacrifice might have prompted the multiple burials. It is possible that in all these cases archaeologists have been excavating the remains of a dark ritual rather than a typical grave site.

The remainder of Wales's population, those not buried in tombs or interred as token cremation deposits, may never have been buried – perhaps their bodies were cast into rivers, or their bones were scattered with ceremony, or perhaps they were kept by the living for similar reasons to those which inspire modern families to retain the ashes of loved ones. Their existence has been wiped from history. And as for those whose remains have survived to the present – scant few compared with those of other periods – none are reconstructable as individuals. Cremation fractures and warps bones, burial in acid soils eats them away leaving only stains. In short, these people remain well hidden: whereas the faces of tomb builders who lived around 3650 BC can be reconstructed, in Wales the people of 3000 BC are lost.

How they lived

The modesty of their burial rites is matched by the invisibility of their settlements. In Wales, no houses survive, nor do farmsteads, fortifications or market places. All that are left are tantalising scratchings in the ground which only the most recent excavators, armed with a battery of scientific techniques, have managed to animate.

At Upper Ninepence near New Radnor in the Walton Basin, Alex Gibson, then of Clwyd-Powys Archaeological Trust, excavated a group of these pits. They had been dug on a low hill set between two streams in sheltered lowlands enclosed by high hills. Over forty pits were found, although only ten could be specifically dated to the years before 3000 BC. Almost all were found over an area about 10 by 20m and each was less than a metre across and at most 33cm deep. Four of them might have been dug in a line, the rest appear randomly scattered.

About a hundred flints were found in the pits as well as sherds from at least twenty pots and charred plant remains. The flints include small scrapers, a serrated knife, piercer and arrowheads, as well as flakes and fragments left over from tool manufacture. Randolph Donahue of Bradford University carried out a detailed study of some of these flints and found that they had been put to a wide range of uses, including slicing plants, cutting meat, scoring bone, shaving wood, and scraping and working dry hides. Stephanie Dudd and Richard Evershed of Bristol University enhanced this picture using gas chromatography to analyse the food residue on some of the pot sherds, showing that some of the pots had been used to cook lamb and beef. The people were also arable farmers, charred plant remains in the pits suggest they grew wheat which they harvested along with some weeds which grew among their crop. The picture which emerges is of a small community going about everyday life, processing and cooking food, and making and using tools.

The quantity of information which has been extracted from the Upper Ninepence assemblage is impressive, but it raises questions. Who were these people and why did they dig these pits and bury their possessions? It is possible that the pits are all that remain of buildings, but there is no evidence to support this view. Instead, Donahue has suggested that they were used to store food which was consumed during the winter, and that they were filled in with rubbish the following year. It is debatable whether burying food in such shallow bowl-shaped pits would have helped to preserve it, but certainly their final contents look like rubbish. Only fragments of pots are found, as though vessels had been broken before burial and the sherds scattered; some of the flint is also burnt, and the charcoal in the pits might suggest that the contents of hearths had been swept into them. But there are easier ways to dispose of rubbish. For instance, waste could simply have been piled up in one place as a midden or compost heap, avoiding the need to dig a pit at all. That pits were dug hints that more was intended than simple rubbish disposal; and it has been suggested in studies of similar sites that such practices may have been an attempt to encourage fertility in the land by feeding the earth with what modern eyes might view as rubbish, but which ancient minds may have regarded as symbolic, or perhaps even actual, fertiliser.

Rustic wares

Even though it cannot be said with certainty that the pits at Upper Ninepence mark the site of a settlement, one piece of evidence suggests that the homes of the pit diggers were not far away: their pottery. Pottery is a relatively heavy and fragile commodity, prone to breakage. Although there is evidence from an earlier time of a trade in pots across southwest England, and some evidence for pots having been transported some distance in Wales in the years after 2000 BC, it seems reasonable to assume that for the most part people expecting to travel far would have carried their possessions in bags made of skin or string, or in baskets, all of which would have been lighter and more flexible. Furthermore, analysis of the clays from which the Upper Ninepence pots were made suggests that they were probably produced locally.

When complete the Upper Ninepence pots were round-bottomed often with thick, heavy rims. They were rustic in quality, especially when compared with some of the fine wares produced a few hundred years before, and were often comprehensively decorated with rough impressions made by bird bones, twisted cord or the fingernail, or by lines incised into the clay, producing an effect similar to that of basketry. Those pots that can be reconstructed are generally larger than a food bowl, suggesting they were used for cooking, serving or storing food.

Radiocarbon dates have shown that this style of pottery began to be made around 3500 BC and continued in use for seven centuries or more. It has been found at over thirty sites across Wales and in adjacent areas, with many of these consisting of groups of pits, similar to those at Upper Ninepence. For example, at least six pits were dug and pottery deposited at Meole Brace near Shrewsbury while pottery was dropped in a single pit at Brynderwen, around 3200 BC or a little before. Pottery of this type is also found at other types of sites in Wales, including caves, as at Daylight Rock in Pembrokeshire and Gop Cave in Flintshire, and in older tombs, such as Capel Garmon in Conwy and Gwernvale in southern Powys.

The quarry face

Coarse pottery and humble flint tools seem a poor range of possessions, and shallow pits and ditches suggest a weak and unambitious age. It is easy to see why early archaeologists regarded these people as savages, or overlooked their existence entirely in their haste to study the older tombs or more recent burial mounds. But so far, only one side of the story has been presented.

While ritual enclosures and cairn-covered graves probably only had meaning for the people in the areas around them, one place in particular had an impact on people's lives across southern and central Britain: Penmaenmawr. This massive buttress of rock once rose over 450m above the north Wales coast. Its core is a volcanic plug of augite granophyre well suited for use as hardcore – a property which has led more recent quarrymen to dig out the heart of the mountain, trimming over 100m off of one peak in the process. But the rock around its south and east sides, as well as on nearby hills has a finer grain, and this made it especially valuable to the people of this time, as a raw material for the manufacture of stone axes.

Around 3000 BC, a group of people sat on the eastern edge of Penmaenmawr, at Graig Lwyd, 'the grey rock'. They were high up on a narrow terrace, with steep screes rising still higher behind them, while before them were views of the north Wales coast, and the Great Orme beyond. They had made a large stone-lined hearth in which a fire roared.

Penmaenmawr (Conwy) from the south.

Much of the peak and northern face of this mountain has been removed by quarrying. Graig Lwyd, the best preserved axe working area, can be seen on the right of this photograph.

The screes provided an abundant supply of raw materials, and the fire kept them warm as they turned rocks over, shifting their weight between their hands, and testing them with a hammerstone to see if they rang true. The good ones they flaked into the rough shape of an axe, a quick job. If the block failed in the making, as many did, the broken pieces were discarded to join the ever growing bed of flakes and debris which littered the ground around, deepening and extending the natural scree. Those which survived were taken to more sheltered spots, where they were polished on a grinding slab over several days. The working area by the hearth was revisited many times; when the area was abandoned the pile of waste debris was more than half a metre deep and covered an area 20 by 40m.

The chipping floor around the hearth was dug by Samuel Hazzledine Warren in 1920 and 1921, and he identified many other stone working sites around the sides of the hill. These have been mapped in more detail by John Llewelyn Williams and David Jenkins, among others, during the 1980s. In total, debris has been found around the entire east side of Graig Lwyd, much of it presumably derived from the working of screes, but in at least one place massive scars on the low cliffs show that the native rock had itself been quarried. Worked debris has also been found on the west side of Penmaenmawr, and on the nearby peaks of Dinas and Garreg Fawr. There is no doubting the importance of this area for the manufacture of axes during this period, although whether this activity was episodic or sustained remains unknown.

This cliff face at Graig Lwyd (Conwy) was probably quarried using hammerstones swung against the rock.

Social networks

Flakes of Graig Lwyd rock have been found by Jane Kenny of Gwynedd Archaeological Trust 14km from the mountain in the postholes of a house built around 3700 BC. These flakes could be explained as the result of local people collecting material for their own use, but rock from Graig Lwyd was also carried much further afield. Before 3000 BC axes were being used over 200km away in the fenland of eastern England. Some of these were eventually buried, much battered and broken, at an enclosure set beside a filled in stream course near Maxey in Cambridgeshire. Graig Lwyd axes have also been found in Yorkshire and across southern England, with a few more appearing on the Isle of Man; they united people from very different areas in a network of trade and exchange.

Graig Lwyd was not the only place to contribute to these networks. Before 3000 BC, rocks gathered from a glacial debris flow on the flanks of the Preseli Hills in Pembrokeshire had also been flaked into axes and carried similar distances, with an example being found at another enclosure built at Hambledon Hill on the edge of the North Dorset Downs.

The traffic was not just one way. Axes made from Cornish, Lake District and southern English rocks are found across Wales. Many have been found churned up by the plough making it impossible to be certain of their date, but a few retain enough of their context to demonstrate the extent and longevity of this exchange network. An axe, brought from the flint-rich lands of southern England, was placed in the chamber of a tomb at Ty-Isaf in southern Powys, possibly around 3600 BC, and fragments from others were buried below the mound of a tomb of similar age at Gwernvale. Axes of pale-greenish rock from Great Langdale in the Lake District have been found at Llandegai, where one was buried blade downward in a small pit, and at the Gwaenysgor settlement site in Flintshire.

In an age when few would consider travelling more than a mile without a car, it is hard to imagine how such long distance networks could have been maintained. The most popular answer has been to assume that axes were exchanged 'down-the-line' from community to community, such that the people using the axes in Cambridgeshire might have had no direct links with people at Graig Lwyd. Indeed they might not even have been aware of the mountains in the west at all and may have valued axes of this foreign rock simply for their hardness and beauty.

Results derived from newly developed scientific techniques suggest that people may have been used to travelling longer distances than this model suggests. One of these

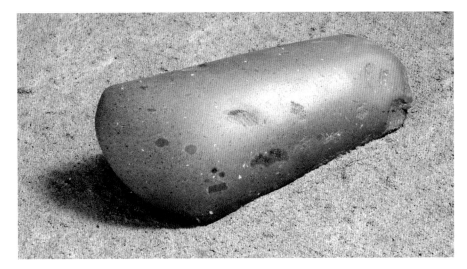

Axe made from Graig Lwyd rock, found in fishing nets on Lavan Sands between Penmaenmawr and Anglesey.

© National Museum of Wales (Kevin Thomas).

Original artefact in private possession. (17.5cm long).

Distribution across Britain of axes made from Graig Lwyd rock (blue diamond), based on data collected by the Implement Petrology Committee.

Despite the number found, very few examples appear in northern Britain, hinting at some barrier to the spread of trade in this direction. It is also striking that Graig Lwyd axes do not appear to have been taken to Ireland with any regularity.

© The National Museum of Wales (Jackie Chadwick, Tony Daly).

techniques capitalises on minute amounts of naturally occurring strontium and oxygen isotopes. Different geologies across Britain are characterised by different ratios of the various types of these isotopes. As the plants and animals which live in each region are eaten and local water drunk, this ratio becomes fixed in human teeth, preserving a signature of the areas in which an individual spent their early years. This new technique has been applied to an adult and three children found in the pit grave at Monkton up Wimborne in Dorset, with intriguing results.

Nodules of Bullhead flint from southern England.

This flint has a characteristic orange rind which can also be seen in the scraper (bottom left). This tool was found in the Walton Basin in Central Powys, some distance from the nearest sources of this type of flint. This seemingly ordinary find provides further evidence of contact between regions.

© The National Museum of Wales (Peter Harp, Jim Wild).

Original artefact housed in the collections of Amgueddfa Cymru – National Museum Wales. (Largest piece, 9cm long).

To paraphrase complexities, their teeth showed that the woman had grown up in the Mendips, some 60km to the northwest of Dorset, and had travelled south to the chalkland, where she met a brother and sister. All three then travelled away from the chalkland where the woman gave birth to a daughter, before returning to Dorset where they all met their end. If this story is typical, then people may have routinely travelled much further at this time than has often been supposed, raising the possibility that people from across southern Britain were aware of places like Graig Lwyd and the Preseli Hills and knew these to be the source of their axes. A few may even have visited these places themselves.

The routes along which these axes were carried are largely speculative, but the topography around the axe production sites provides some basic insights, particularly in the mountainous country around Graig Lwyd. From here the valleys of the Rivers Conwy and Clwyd offer a route to the Cheshire Plain from where axes could have been passed in any direction. Alternatively, seafarers might have beached their boats at the base of the mountain and carried axes away using a waterborne route. A sea route is also likely to have been important in carrying axes east from Pembrokeshire and north from Cornish production sites.

If axes were carried great distances, doubtless other goods were, although only the most durable items survive as proof of this. Returning to Upper Ninepence, here although the local people probably made pots from clay found in their immediate area, they also added fragments of schist, a rock which is found over 50km away near the Wrekin in Shropshire, or in the Malvern Hills of Worcestershire. This schist would have made the pots more durable, but many more easily obtainable materials would have served the same purpose. Since it is likely that the potters of the Walton Basin used local clays, either they had chanced upon fragments of schist within the local sandstones, or they had a strong desire for this particular rock, and a willingness to travel or trade to get it. Another hint that people in this area had links with the wider world comes from a single scraper made from an unusual flint, known as Bullhead flint. This is found in parts of Essex, Berkshire, Kent and Dorset, although again the possibility of fragments of material with a similar appearance being present in local glacially-derived deposits cannot be ruled out.

Stone tools and beautiful things

Although the colour of the Bullhead flint scraper from Upper Ninepence is unusual its form is matched by that of hundreds of other scrapers found in all parts of Wales. These, along with flint knives, boring tools, arrowheads and sharp-edged flakes were workaday tools as they had been in one form or another for millennia, and as they

Hoard of flint flakes found at Penmachno (Conwy) in 1928.

The high quality of these large flakes suggests they were brought to Wales from the chalklands of southern or eastern England, or northeast Ireland. Ireland is the closest of these potential sources.

© The National Museum of Wales (Jim Wild).

Original artefacts housed in the collections of Amgueddfa Cymru – National Museum Wales. (Average length 10-11cm).

would be until the end of the period covered by this book. In skilled hands they were quick to produce; more problematic was the acquisition of the raw material.

Flint is common in the chalklands of southern England and east Yorkshire and can also be found as outcrops in parts of northeast Ireland. In Wales it is rarer, being found in earth moved by glaciers from flint-rich areas, or on the coast to which the tides have rolled it. This pebble flint is often small and battered – no doubt an impoverished resource in the eyes of those who lived on the chalk and those who traded better quality flint into the borderlands of Wales.

Not all flint was used for workaday purposes. One piece found at Maesmor in Denbighshire in 1840 was crafted for hundreds of hours to make the head of a mace small enough to be cupped in the hand, but one of the finest examples of contemporary stone carving to have been found in Britain.

The immense skill and effort that went in to this piece are obvious, and yet there was no obvious need for such time-consuming embellishment. Were it intended for use as a war club, then even a simple piece of wood would have served the same purpose. Likewise, there were simpler ways of making a tool to serve as a hammer. More likely, this was intended to display the power of its owner – a weapon in a battle for prestige, rather than a war of conquest. Since none of the other mace heads found in Wales can compare to its beauty and craftsmanship it is a battle which its owner may well have won.

The diamond design on this mace head was widespread at this time and is well-known on flint mace heads from Quarnford in Staffordshire, Airdens in the Scottish Highlands and Urquhart in Moray. A still more elaborate example has been found in the chamber of a passage tomb at Knowth in Ireland which is carved with a face – the facetted pattern suggesting hair. All of these mirror other mace heads made from antler, some of which have been radiocarbon dated by Roy Loveday and Alex Gibson to the centuries around 3000 BC.

Mace heads were not the only non-utilitarian items to be desired at this time: narrow strips of stone less than 10cm long and perforated by a lozenge-shaped hole were also widespread. Only two finished

Mace head found at Maesmor (Denbighshire).

This was made from a large and flawless piece of flint. First, the rough shape of the mace flaked from the flint, a chance to test the rock with well aimed blows from a hammer. Then came the time consuming task of drilling a 48mm deep hole, 18mm in diameter, using only wood, stone and abrasive sand. This alone was a colossal task, and it was followed by another still larger: the carving of a fine filigree of grooves around the outside to create the facetted pattern. This resulted in the only obvious flaw in the craftsman's work. Although complete, there is a slight mismatch in the design where the first groove does not quite meet the final one.

© The National Museum of Wales (Kevin Thomas).

Original artefact in the collections of The National Museum of Scotland, currently on loan to Amgueddfa Cymru – National Museum Wales. (7.6cm long).

examples are known from Wales, both found at Gop Cave. Their finder, William Boyd Dawkins, called them belt-sliders following a convention which had been accepted since the 1850s. The name was chosen to reflect the only obvious function which could be imagined – to hold a belt or sash in place – with support for this hypothesis coming from the discovery of examples close to the hips of skeletons.

As well as suggesting that the dead of 3000 BC, both men and women, were buried wearing clothes that required belts to fasten them, there is another side to the belt-slider which suggests that it may also have served as a badge of some kind, affiliating its owner with a specific cultural tradition. For not only were belt-sliders made to a distinctive shape, but they were also consistently made from a dark stone which could take a fine polish, typically jet or shale. Sadly, the Gop Cave belt-sliders have been lost, but since scientific work by Alison Sheridan and Mary Davis has identified many belt-sliders as being of jet, it seems reasonable to follow Boyd Dawkins in identifying these examples as either being of jet or shale.

Jet is found on the Yorkshire coast near Whitby, over 200km from Gop Cave, and it may seem surprising that it was brought so far to a land which has no shortage of stone. The reason for its value may have been its rare electrostatic properties – when rubbed it can literally make the hair stand up, an ability which may have seemed magical at the time – or perhaps it was valued for its unusual rich black lustre. Those who saw the people around Gop Cave wearing belt-sliders would probably have recognised them as important and well-connected.

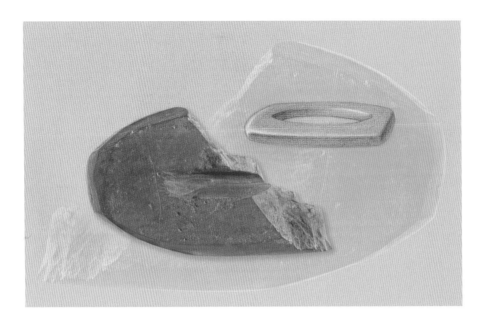

The prestige that could be had from owning a jet belt-slider may provide an explanation for a related discovery made at the other end of Wales over a century later. In 1999 Mike Hamilton, then of Newport University, excavated on the coast at Ogmore-by-Sea in Glamorgan. Finds included flints and pot sherds as well as several worked fragments of a black stone, including an unfinished belt-slider, broken across the beginnings of the perforation. This suggests that people collected pieces of lignite and cannel coal, both jet-like materials, washed up on the shore, and crafted them into artefacts reminiscent of the prestigious examples derived from Yorkshire. Either the Ogmore-by-Sea belt-slider was intended to suggest its owners had far-flung cultural connections they did not in fact possess, or it was simply the black colour which was important to the owners of some belt-sliders, rather than the exact type of stone used.

The dark corners of Wales

This then is the evidence which survives for life in Wales in the years around 3000 BC. In the northwest of the country, Wales brushed with a millennia-old tradition of passage tomb burial, linking it with communities observing similar practices along the Atlantic coastline of Europe. While this was a short-lived experiment in internationalism, people across Wales remained a part of Britain-wide networks made physical through jet belt-sliders and stone axes. Then there is the other evidence which indicate links between communities here and in neighbouring areas: the style of pottery, the pit graves and the circular enclosures. Indeed there is little evidence upon which to base a suggestion that the people in Wales viewed themselves as a separate and definable group of people. One might go further still with the observation that there is scarcely sufficient evidence with which to demonstrate that the country was completely occupied at all. The best of the evidence has been presented here and yet it has left whole regions untouched – including some which showed ample evidence for occupation in previous and successive times, such as southwest Wales, much of Glamorgan, Monmouthshire and adjacent uplands. But people were certainly present in at least some of these places; they reveal themselves even though they built no monuments and hid away both their living spaces and their dead.

On the Black Mountain and in the Brecon Beacons environmental information is stored in multi-layered peat bogs. Peat formation traps the pollen of plants which grow in the vicinity of bogs, sealing them below ever-deepening layers of partially rotted plant material. By carefully excavating a column of peat, identifying the pollen contained in each layer and then radiocarbon dating the sequence, an area's environmental history can be built up. When complete these sequences generally show Ice Age tundra giving way to shrubs and then to rapidly growing trees which in turn give way to slower growing deciduous woodland. Often traces of other events are preserved in the peat.

At Nant Helen, just south of the Black Mountain, the pollen record showed a marked decline in the number of birch trees around 3000 BC, accompanied by a concentration of charcoal. It is possible that this charcoal results from a lightning strike causing a fire which spread across the hillside, but charcoal is a frequent find in peat bogs of this time – more likely it is evidence of human activity, perhaps campfires, possibly deliberate clearance of the forest. Contemporary charcoal from the burning of heather has also been found on the Black Mountain itself at Waun Fignen Felen, and on the coast at Goldcliff near Newport. A small bog called

Abercynafon, on the flanks of the Brecon Beacons, contained more revealing evidence still. Here deciduous woodland was cleared around 3000 BC, making room for open ground in which grew weeds. Some of the wood still survives, and marks upon it have been interpreted by its discoverer, Caroline Earwood, as evidence that it had been worked by human hands.

The people who felled these trees, and cut and burnt the wood have left no other mark, their epitaph just a whispered statement blown into the pollen sequence of a peat bog. A fitting motif for an age where people seem to have hid their daily lives from history.

Excavation of an area of prehistoric woodland at Abercynafon (southern Powys), following the site's discovery by forestry workers in 1994.

© The National Museum of Wales.

2900 – 2500 BC.
An insular folk

After the abandonment of the passage tombs people in both Britain and Ireland seem not to have been greatly influenced by trends in mainland Europe. It is as though the cultural concerns current around 3000 BC provided sufficient fuel without the need to look further afield. But while Britain experimented with its cultural isolation, Europe did not stand still; fresh ideas and new technologies swept across the continent in the years between 2900 and 2500 BC. Although these did not break upon the shores of Britain and Ireland until after this period, when they did so it was with such long term effect that their genesis is worth recording here as a counterpoint to Wales's own story. Two of these major themes were material – metal and a style of pottery known as 'Beaker pots' – and one cultural – a burial rite which honoured the individual after death.

The coming change

Metals had been used in parts of Europe since the sixth millennium BC. Beginning in the Balkans, raw nuggets of native copper were used, then rich seams of ore were exploited. Copper was mined in Bulgaria from about 5500 BC, and the products were traded far beyond the mines, encouraging the exploitation of other sources. By 3000 BC copper was being worked in southern Spain and Portugal, and around the Alps. Most famously, at this time, the 'Ice Man' attempted to cross these mountains carrying among his possessions a copper axe. In northern Europe, copper trinkets were occasionally placed in graves, but this new material does not seem to have been recognised as a life-changing innovation – either that or the secrets of its productions were closely guarded by communities further south. For people living in what is now Wales, mineral ores were to remain a colourful curiosity for some centuries to come.

The discovery of metallurgy was a giant technological leap and, regardless of how it was viewed at the time, the practical benefits of metal tools make it easy to rationalise their general adoption in southern Europe. The reason for the other material change which swept Europe in this period, the adoption of Beaker pottery, is altogether harder to grasp.

Location of sites in Wales mentioned in this chapter.

1 Bryn Celli Ddu
2 Bryn yr Hen Bobl
3 Capel Eithin
4 Dyffryn Lane
5 Gop
6 Graig Lwyd
7 Hendre
8 Hindwell
9 Lithalun Quarry
10 Llandegai
11 Lligwy
12 Meusydd
13 New Radnor
14 Orchid Cave
15 Parc Bryn Cegin
16 Pentrefoelas
17 Preseli Hills
18 Tooth Cave
19 Trefeglwys
20 Trelystan
21 Ty-Isaf
22 Upper Ninepence
23 Vaynor Farm
24 Walton.

© The National Museum of Wales (Jackie Chadwick, Tony Daly).

Pots in this style were first made in Mediterranean Europe, probably in the Iberian peninsula. Beakers are generally tall, bell shaped, and ornately decorated, often with lines or zigzags impressed with cord or comb. Some of the earliest dated examples come from Atalayuela in northern Spain. Here, at some time between 2900 and 2600 BC, seventy to eighty bodies were piled into a pit, along with the remains of nine Beakers, bone and copper pins, buttons and arrowheads, amongst other grave goods. Beaker pottery also appears around this time at fortified settlements such as Zambujal in Portugal where it is again linked with copper working. In this region the new mix of copper working and fortification suggests a society of haves and have-nots, with Beaker pottery playing some part in expressing this disunity. It is harder to see why the Beaker design should have resonated so clearly with people as far afield as southern Scandinavia, Italy, Hungary, and Morocco, leading to its adoption in these areas, and why, in the years after 2500 BC, it should have become so widespread in Britain and Ireland.

The trend towards burying the dead as individuals seems to have had its genesis in another part of Europe. While communities in many regions had used this funerary rite before 2900 BC, it is only around this time that the practice became more widespread, beginning perhaps in central or eastern Europe. A cemetery at Čachovice in northwest Bohemia provides a good example. Here, some time after 2900 BC, fifty-nine graves were dug, each containing a single skeleton of a man, woman or child accompanied by items including pottery, stone tools and a few items of jewellery such as copper beads, earrings and a necklace. Similar evidence is found across northern and central Europe, suggesting that people retained something of their individuality in death, rather than their remains becoming mixed with those of others to form generic ancestors for a community. Later burials at Čachovice continue this theme, but by this time Beaker pottery was being placed with the dead. This linking of Beaker pottery and the burial of individuals was to become common across northwest Europe.

There is considerable debate as to how and why these changes spread. Was it the result of migrating communities, or of separate peoples adopting practices begun by their neighbours? In Britain, as yet unaffected by these changes, a more important question than how these changes were occurring may well have been: what will they mean for us? The answer was not to come until around 2400 BC, when these tides of change broke across Britain and Ireland. But these were events to be faced by later generations. For now, Wales had a cultural life of its own.

Clearing up after dinner

This chapter covers about 400 years of life in Wales – at least twenty generations. Nearly long enough to take us back to the reign of Queen Elizabeth I. In a society without writing, this span of time would have been too great for accurate memory, no matter how carefully histories were passed to descendants in story, song or ritual. By 2600 BC, the names of the people buried in Bryn Celli Ddu or in Gop Cave or at Trelystan were forgotten or at best misremembered; likewise, the original purpose of the enclosure at Llandegai and similar sites was probably also lost. Where such sites were still visible on the ground, they may well have been woven into the fabric of myths and campfire stories.

Nowhere is this folklore of former times more likely than in the Walton Basin, where a succession of monuments was built over the course of a thousand years. Much of this will be discussed towards the end of this chapter, but here attention focuses on a more modest succession which can be demonstrated in the same area at Upper Ninepence.

The area around the Upper Ninepence pits described in the previous chapter was abandoned, perhaps for a few decades after 2900 BC, possibly for much longer; when it was reoccupied around 2800 BC, the nature of the settlement was very similar to that which had gone before, just a scatter of pits and at least one circle of small holes where stakes formed the outer frame of a 6m diameter house with a hearth at its centre. The site continued to be occupied for some time as, after this house went out of use, a ditch was dug across the ground it occupied, and more pits were dug, around 2600 BC.

As far as is known, the way of life of the people who dug these new pits also seems to have differed only in detail from that described previously.

The wear on flint tools used in this more recent occupation suggests that the community at Upper Ninepence was now focused on the processing of hides, to the exclusion of some of the other chores that are evident earlier. Possibly they

Chisel-shaped arrowheads from Upper Ninepence (central Powys).

These unlikely arrowheads may not have been sharp enough to inflict a mortal wound on impact, but the broad cut they made may have led to death by blood-loss soon after.

© National Museum of Wales (Kevin Thomas).

Original artefacts housed in the collections of Amgueddfa Cymru – National Museum Wales. (Longest example, 4cm).

conducted these other activities elsewhere, perhaps other parts of the community undertook them on their behalf. Their diet had also changed. From cooking lamb, beef, or perhaps dairy products, they had begun to cook pig – again there is no evidence for leafy vegetables in the residues that were absorbed into the sides of their pots, and now even less evidence for cereals in the charred material found in the fills of the pits. This is surprising. As Dale Serjeantson has noted, the diet of peasants in medieval Britain was typically a pottage of cereal and vegetables stewed with old bones, and a similar diet would seem likely at this time. Furthermore, since salt was not produced on a large scale, if an animal was killed it would have to have been smoked or consumed rapidly – an opportunity for people to gather and share in the sacrifice of an animal, strengthening social bonds and tightening the interdependence of communities.

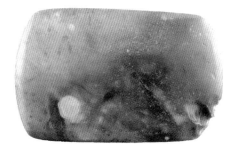

New art from ancient sources

The style of pots in which pig meat was boiled or stewed at Upper Ninepence marked another change between the lives of the people of 3000 BC and now. The new vessels ranged in size from small bowls to large tubs which could have held a substantial amount. The inside of the largest was coated with a thick crust, suggesting it had been left on a fire and its contents burnt, while the smaller, open-mouthed vessels seem suited for a use as communal serving bowls; but it is the decoration on the pots which is especially interesting.

The impressed decoration common to previous generations was now much rarer. Instead most designs were incised into the clay, creating diagonal and zigzag lines, sometimes forming diamond shapes. In other cases, the pot's surface was divided by vertical ribs of clay stuck to the outside of the vessel. Similar pots, in a style known to archaeologists as Grooved Ware, are found at other sites in Wales and indeed across Britain and Ireland, with the full range of the decorative repertoire also including occasional spirals. For the potter of 2900 BC, this was a new design repertoire, but to the people of 3000 BC it would have been very familiar, albeit in another context: the dark world of the passage tombs.

Decoration on Grooved Ware pots from Wales, including examples of designs used at Lligwy (Anglesey), Trelystan (northern Powys), and Upp Ninepence (central Powys).

© The National Museum of Wales (Tony Daly).

By 2900 BC, Wales's passage tombs were probably long closed and abandoned, and their carved art is unlikely to have offered a visible inspiration to later generations. But further afield the art style would still have been visible. In Ireland, tombs like Knowth and Newgrange are surrounded by elaborately decorated kerb stones and here, although the tombs may have been abandoned, occupation continued around them. In Orkney, another focus of passage tomb construction, the chronology of tomb use is less clear, but once again the land around the tombs continued to be occupied after 3000 BC.

It seems likely that it was in these areas that potters first began to base their designs on passage tomb art. This change illustrates more than just a fickle desire for new pots, rather it reflects a wider shift in the nature of society. Previously, this abstract art had been hidden away inside tombs to which few would have had access, and when it was made public, as on the kerbstones at Newgrange and Knowth, it was still linked with the ritualised and obscure practices implied by these canvasses. In translating it on to cooking pots and serving bowls, potters made the style available to all and, from being associated with rituals and death, it became tied to food and life.

Hearth and home

One of the sites where this link can best be seen is at Trelystan. By 2600 BC two houses had been built on either side of the earlier pit grave. Both were delineated by a rough circle of stakes, four to five metres in diameter, presumably with wattle and daub joining them. No evidence survives to confirm the style of roof on these houses, with the excavator, Bill Britnell, favouring a roof set on top of the uprights, while Alex Gibson has proposed that the stakes may have propped up a conical roof which rested on the ground at its outer edges.

A number of pits cut the floor of these houses and at their centre were square hearths, lined with stone slabs held upright in slots cut into the floor. The pits were probably used for storing food and equipment, or for cooking: one contained fragments of two Grooved Ware pots, some flint, including a scraper, and some burnt bone. One of these houses was occupied long enough for a hearth stone to be moved and possibly for a pit to be filled in and replaced by another, but even this is unlikely to reflect more than a generation of occupation. Damp soils and high winds would have worn down these structures and the slight evidence for the rebuilding of one of the walls would not have delayed the inevitable for long. Even so, here is

The houses found on either side of the pit grave at Trelystan (northern Powys).

Alex Gibson has shown that the surviving evidence from the houses can be interpreted in two ways resulting in quite different structures, as seen here.

© The National Museum of Wales (Tony Daly).

evidence for family-sized dwellings where an ancient art of death was comfortably accepted within the domestic milieu of pots and pans.

Similarly built structures were erected as far afield as Dorset and Orkney, demonstrating once again how ephemeral evidence can provide a clue to island-wide trends. Mike Parker Pearson who has excavated a number of houses at Durrington Walls in Wiltshire has remarked on their archaeological fragility – a single ploughing would be enough to destroy them completely – and this is likely to have been the fate of many built in Wales. Here may be another explanation for a number of sites where pits have been found containing Grooved Ware, but without surrounding structures, for example, at Parc Bryn Cegin and Llandegai (both in Gwynedd), Capel Eithin on Anglesey, and at Hendre in Flintshire. Perhaps, as at Trelystan, these pots were the sweepings from hearths and houses which have since been lost to erosion or the plough.

Religious sentiments

Like the Grooved Ware art style, the design of monuments built at this time can also be traced back to 3000 BC. With the exception of the monument at Stonehenge, there is nothing to suggest that the precisely circular enclosures built around the turn of the millennium remained in use for long and it is likely that much of their role was incorporated into a new type of monument known to archaeologists as the henge. This classification was developed in the 1930s and is now applied to roughly circular enclosures of varying sizes where the bank was built outside the ditch, reversing the earlier arrangement of these two elements and providing, by implication, the clearest evidence that henges served as ceremonial centres.

By definition, an enclosure is designed to seal off an area, with the majority of likely functions – field, stockade, fortification – emphasising the desire to keep things out. By setting the bank outside the ditch, the builders of henges seem to have been more interested in keeping things in, and perhaps also in providing a raised area from which people could witness events in the interior while the ditch prevented them from participating themselves.

Henges were first built around 2900 BC, with the Stones of Stenness on Orkney, a 55m diameter henge with a massive 2m deep ditch, being an early example. At the other end of Britain, and a little later, a 40 to 50m diameter henge was built with a 2.5m deep ditch at Coneybury in Wiltshire. But the majority of henges seem to have been built some time after this date, and in Wales only one has produced evidence suggesting that it might be early: the Llandegai henge.

The Llandegai henge is similar in size to the earlier enclosure, as though its builders were refreshing a focal point for their community in more contemporary form. It is not known for certain when building work was undertaken – the only material to be dated from the ditch did not come from the base – but a scatter of pits inside the monument may be contemporary with its use. One of these, which was dug

Group of prehistoric monuments at Llandegai (Gwynedd).

The ditch of the Llandegai henge appears as the dark circle at the top of this aerial photograph. The earlier, and very similar, circular enclosure is closer to the camera.

Llandegai is a place with strategic significance. The Rivers Cegin and Ogwen flow past it, with the course of the latter providing the start of a route into Snowdonia and, through mountain passes and valley courses, to the English lowlands – a route now followed by the line of the modern A5 road. It is also positioned within reach of the North Wales coast.

© Cambridge University Collection of Air Photographs.

around 2800 BC, was set just beyond the edge of the henge bank hinting that this had already been built by this time. The nature of the rituals conducted inside the Llandegai henge will always remain obscure, but there is nothing to suggest that the link with the dead, so clear at the earlier enclosure, was perpetuated at this new monument. Other henges in Wales such as Dyffryn Lane in northern Powys and Vaynor Farm in Carmarthenshire were either built, or continued in use, after the period covered by this chapter, so discussion of these sites is reserved for later.

Keeping up with old friends

Another pit inside the Llandegai henge held a range of flint tools, as well as the blade of an axe and flakes made from Graig Lwyd rock. The axe head had broken across its middle and a clear fracture line extended down its length suggesting that it had broken during use. While it is not known why these pieces were buried – was it rubbish clearance or ritual? – they are sufficient to demonstrate a continued interest in the stone found on the nearby mountain.

It is even possible that the same stretch of mountainside that was used as a workshop around 3000 BC was still in use, since Hazzledine Warren discovered a strange stone plaque there when he was excavating in 1920. This plaque, which is only about the size of a pocket notebook, has been carefully carved with a design which is unmistakably 'Grooved Ware'. The reverse of this piece has also been cut with a metal tool, raising the possibility that it was found at another location by more recent, perhaps even nineteenth-century, workmen and used as a test piece for a time before being abandoned while these men walked to the Graig Lwyd quarries.

The passing of axes beyond Wales also continued. An axe from Graig Lwyd was placed with other finds in a pit at Firtree Field in Dorset around 2700 BC, while a few hundred metres away and some time later, an axe produced from the loose rocks on the flanks of the Preseli Hills was deposited in the infilled ditch of a henge on Wyke Down. Graig Lwyd axes dating to this general period have also been found in the Avebury and Stonehenge areas of Wiltshire, while the eastern extent of these exchange networks is indicated by their presence in pits at Barholm in Lincolnshire.

Graig Lwyd axe in a pit at Firtree Field (Dorset).

This pit was one of several found at this site. Others contained such finds as flint tools, a hammerstone and a boar's tusk.

© Martin Green.

A home for giants

Much of the evidence presented in this chapter suggests the slow development of ancient themes. Perhaps the least welcome of all these, from an archaeological perspective, is the continued dearth of burial ritual up to 2500 BC.

Grave pits ceased to be dug, and no obvious burial tradition took their place. Once again a few bodies were placed in old burial chambers, for example at Ty-Isaf in southern Powys, Bryn yr Hen Bobl on Anglesey, and Druid's Stoke in Gloucestershire, suggesting a continued desire to link with the past. The occasional burial was also placed in a cave, as at Orchid Cave in Flintshire, and possibly Tooth Cave on Gower, but once more the lack of evidence suggests that the dead were not afforded lasting memorials. More likely their remains were burnt and scattered, just smoke and dust. The missing dead and the scarcity of settlement evidence might give the sense that Wales was an empty land at this time. Yet people were present and they were capable of great works requiring the marshalling of large numbers of people as important discoveries have shown in recent years.

In July 1975, aerial photographer J K St Joseph was flying sorties in the Welsh Marches looking for archaeological sites. One flight took him over the Walton Basin, where he spotted a 400m long arc of pits, met by two parallel lines suggesting an entrance approach, over 50m long, about 6m wide and composed of at least ten pairs of posts. If this arc were to be continued to form a full enclosure he calculated that it would be over 300m in diameter and contain about four hectares, although it is just as likely that it was only ever just an arc, its other sides formed by the line of the Summergil and Riddings Brooks.

The enclosure reminded St Joseph of a very similar site he had discovered while flying above Meldon Bridge in Peeblesshire in the early 1960s and indeed in 1978 he published his discovery of a third site of the same design at Forteviot in Perthshire. The presence of such similar monuments separated by such distances is striking and it suggests that whole communities were motivated by a need to emulate the grand designs of others – even those far beyond their everyday sphere of contacts.

The late Glyn Owen of Clwyd-Powys Archaeological Trust excavated a single pit along the line of the Walton enclosure's palisade wall in 1998. Another was excavated by Nigel Jones in 2010. Owen's pit was 1.25m deep and had held a 0.6m diameter post probably made of oak. These excavations were too small to allow reconstruction of the enclosure, but larger scale work has been carried out at Meldon Bridge. At this Scottish site, the posts were connected by cladding to form a solid front, with the interior being used for rituals and burial rites, but the structure probably only stood for a century before its oak timbers rotted away. There seems no reason to believe that the situation was greatly different at the Walton enclosure.

This wall of timber would have confronted anyone travelling east, down from the uplands of the Radnor Forest. To pass into its interior the traveller would probably have had to walk down the avenue entranceway, their world enclosed by its massive timbers until they reached the open expanse of the interior. For a people more used to open spaces and small settlements it must have been a powerful experience.

The Walton enclosure is just the start of the story. In 1992, Cadw funded a project to review the archaeology of the Walton Basin and, as part of this, Alex Gibson took a plane up over the area. Weather was poor and his pilot was forced to fly an unusual path into the basin. In doing so, he spotted another enclosure at Hindwell, which he subsequently explored through geophysics and excavation. His discovery was even more remarkable than the one made by St Joseph.

The Hindwell enclosure was an oval, delineated by around 1,400 posts, each about 0.8m in diameter and perhaps 8m tall. If these uprights were ever joined by timber cladding then about 12,000 tonnes of wood would have been needed. In total the builders enclosed around 34 hectares behind a wall over two kilometres in length. For comparison, millennia later the Romans built marching camps and a fort in the basin; the largest of these covers only half the area of the Hindwell enclosure and yet was capable of housing 12–13,000 men.

Radiocarbon dates from the Hindwell enclosure suggest it was built between 2700 and 2500 BC, the Walton enclosure was built just a few hundred metres away probably some time after this. Although the span of time which separated their building is uncertain it is likely that for a while at least, both enclosures stood side by side, one in decay, the other newly raised.

Construction of these two vast works would have strained both the human and natural resources of the area. Assuming that a hectare of mature wood could have produced around thirty trees with straight trunks about 20m tall then at least 23 hectares of mature woodland would have had to be deforested during the construction of this single enclosure. Dave Chapman of Ancient Arts suggests that the easiest way to fell these would have been to build a fire around their base and burn through them, using a technique employed more recently by North American Indians, rather than expend the effort involved in cutting them down; but still there would have been an enormous amount of effort involved in cutting off side branches

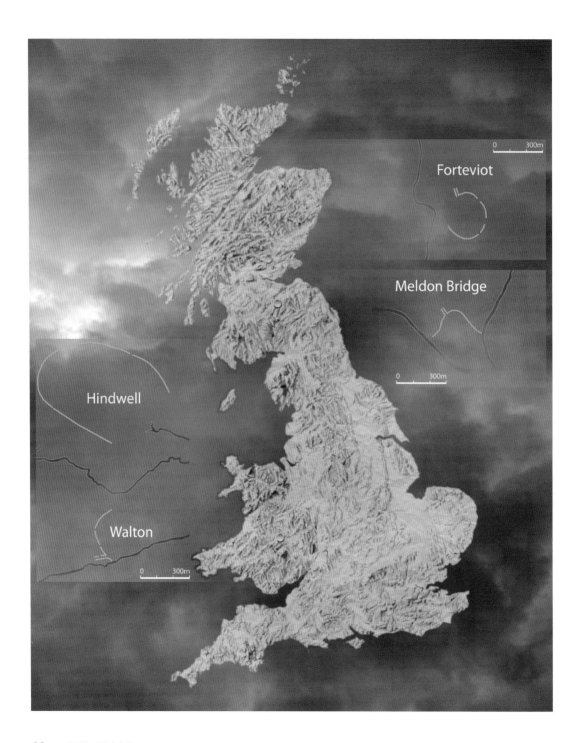

Forteviot

0   300m

Meldon Bridge

0   300m

Hindwell

Walton

0   300m

and trimming posts. Much of this would have been undertaken with stone axes, and it is reasonable to assume that large numbers of broken stone axe heads would be found in the area where this work was carried out. Extensive walking of the basin by Chris Dunn in the 1960s located over twenty axe fragments on the higher ground north of the enclosures and it is tempting to see these as debris from tree felling.

Calculations by Gibson suggest that the Walton Basin may have supported around 500 people, of whom 100 may have been fit for the challenge of enclosure building. If these people had been available for 200 days a year it would have taken them over 160 days just to dig the pits into which the posts would slot. A further 23 days would have been needed to fell and trim the trees, then at least another 70 to drag the posts into position, more if the trees were brought from a distance. If the wall had indeed been clad to form a solid barrier, then a further 340 days will have been needed to produce the planks and the ropes to secure them. Even with the full workforce of the basin working on the project, it would have taken over three years to build the Hindwell enclosure – and then of course there was the building of the Walton enclosure to the south.

Gibson has suggested that some of the hard labour of hauling the four-tonne posts may have been done by cattle as beasts of burden. Certainly, cattle were used to pull wagons in central Europe by 2900 BC and it would be surprising if they were not also used to save labour where possible. But while the details of the construction methods will always remain elusive, the sheer commitment needed to build these great works is evident. The scale of the Hindwell enclosure is completely out of step with any other contemporary monument in Wales, or in the rest of Britain and Ireland.

The function of these two neighbouring enclosures remains enigmatic. Were they defended places? Were they the sites of markets? Or were they religious sites? The remains themselves give little away. The entrance avenue at the Walton enclosure has already been noted. At Hindwell, the west side of the enclosure was pierced by a two metre wide gap flanked by massive timber posts – a narrow entrance given the scale of the monument. But no obviously contemporary internal features or significant scatters of flint tools have been found within the enclosure. In contrast, dense scatters of flint on a ridge just 300m to the north, and the evidence from Upper Ninepence which sits on this ridge, suggests that the people lived here and not within the enclosure.

Although it will never be known for certain why the builders felt compelled to erect these enclosures, some attempt at explanation can be made as to why this area was chosen for their project. Today, the Walton Basin is cut by the A44, which links Aberystwyth to Oxford along a natural route from the uplands of Wales to the English lowlands. Positioned at the junction of these two landscape blocks, the Walton Basin provides a natural meeting place for communities in both areas, and as such has both strategic and economic importance. These factors were recognised in the middle ages when a new town, 'New Radnor' was built by the Marcher Lords, forming a focal point for trade in the area. The Romans also visited the basin repeatedly, leading armies through it and then building a fort within it. It is likely that the earlier enclosure builders of the Walton Basin were exploiting the same strategic benefits offered by this sheltered junction of uplands and lowlands.

Although the structures they built were magnificent, they were also transitory. Despite deliberate attempts to stop the wall posts rotting by charring their bases, they would have decayed with time. At Walton the cladding would have quickly fallen, with the uprights following them after about 150 years. At Hindwell, the larger posts would have lasted longer, but their end was inevitable, and there is no evidence that they were replaced. While the outline of these monuments may still have been visible for generations after – indeed part of the perimeter of the Hindwell enclosure is still followed by the modern road – their practical value as structures was probably in decline within a few centuries.

Viewed across the timescale of this book, enclosure building in the Walton Basin was a short-lived enterprise and one which was not continued after this brief explosive episode. Indeed, the later archaeology of the area does not appear markedly different from that found in neighbouring parts. What drove the builders to their great works and what caused their descendants to abandon their ambitions are two of the great questions for those studying this period.

Moving mountains

While only slight surface traces survive of the Walton enclosures, the other great endeavour known from this time is still very much in evidence at one of the world's most visited prehistoric sites, Stonehenge in Wiltshire. Here, within the outer circle of massive sarsen stones can be seen a collection of about thirty so-called 'bluestones', smaller uprights arranged in a circle and a horseshoe. Originally there may have been over eighty of these stones at Stonehenge, with archaeologists traditionally assuming that they were erected around 2500 BC.

Geoffrey of Monmouth, the twelfth-century writer, was the first to record a belief that these bluestones were not local to Wiltshire: he attributed their origin to

Ireland and the hand of Merlin. Throughout the nineteenth century various scholars presented their own thoughts on the subject and, with the benefit of a greater degree of geological expertise, possible sources were suggested in Ireland, Shropshire, the Mendips, North Wales, Cumbria, Devon, and Cornwall. H H Thomas, a geologist working in southwest Wales, was the first to explore seriously the possibility that the bluestones were derived from outcrops in the Preseli Hills area, publishing his conclusions in 1923. Subsequent work has focused the search still more, with suggestions that some of the stones came from specific outcrops in a two kilometre area, including Carn Menyn and Carnalw, while another stone has been sourced by Richard Bevins and Rob Ixer to Pont Saeson, just north of the Preseli

Two of the Preseli bluestones at Stonehenge, photographed in front of the larger sarsen stones which are derived from a source in Wiltshire.

© Tim Darvill.

Hills. Rob Ixer and Peter Turner have also suggested that the Altar Stone at Stonehenge was derived from the Old Red Sandstone Senni Beds which can be found from west of Kidwelly through South Wales and the Borders. So while the detailed provenance of the Stonehenge stones will undoubtedly continue to be refined by future generations, there is no doubt that Wales is intimately bound up with the story.

More hotly debated than the source of the stones has been the mechanism by which they came to be on Salisbury Plain. At the start of the twentieth century it was generally assumed that they arrived at their present location by the hand of man, but in 1901 J W Judd suggested it was more likely that they were carried by glaciers which spread south before melting and dropping the stones they had picked up along the way. One key point militates against this view: despite considerable searching, there is no widely accepted evidence for glaciers reaching Salisbury Plain. Certainly glaciers may have carried the stones part of the way – research by Richard Bevins has shown that glacially transported stones from Ramsey Island in Pembrokeshire are known as far east as the Vale of Glamorgan – but no suitable sized blocks of Preseli bluestone have yet been found eroding from the boulder clays of southeast Wales. While debate continues, at present it seems more likely to the author that the builders of Stonehenge acquired their stones from the Preseli Hills themselves.

Here, large numbers of rock spears break the horizon giving the hilltop a jagged crown, and it is easy to visualise a suitable column being selected from among the jumble. Indeed, intensive survey by Geoff Wainwright of the Society of Antiquaries of London and Tim Darvill of Bournemouth University has located cleared areas on Carn Menyn, suggesting the routes by which these columns were dragged from the outcrops. Although no certain date can be attributed to these features, this is exactly the kind of evidence that would be expected from the gathering and initial working of the stones from Stonehenge.

Much has been written about the route that would have been followed in carrying the stones to Wiltshire. Richard Bevins and Rob Ixer's recent work suggests that some were transported from north of the Preseli Hills, but most attention has, to date, focused on potential routes that may have been followed from the peaks of the Preseli's themselves. The most detailed study of the likely routes from this location was undertaken in the 1950s by Richard Atkinson, later of Cardiff University. In his view transportation would have been most easily accomplished by water, with the

Carn Menyn, Preseli Hills (Pembrokeshire).

The dolerites that form the spine of these hills naturally erode into sharp pillars. From a distance the hilltop looks as though it has been deliberately fortified by a crown of stones.

© The National Museum of Wales (Steve Burrow).

A bluestone pillar, Carn Menyn, Preseli Hills (Pembrokeshire).

It looks as though this pillar was deliberately set in this position by workmen who then accidentally broke it while pecking at its sides with hammerstones. But when did this occur: 4,500 years ago during preparations for Stonehenge, or two hundred years ago while preparing a gatepost?

© The National Museum of Wales (Steve Burrow).

stones, each weighing up to four tonnes, being dragged to Milford Haven, where they were placed on rafts and paddled up the Severn Estuary, into the Bristol Avon. From there to Salisbury Plain, they would have been ferried by river as much as possible to minimise the effort of haulage – a task which may have required as many as twenty people per stone. To minimise this effort still further, it has also been argued that a seaborne route around Cornwall may have been taken, albeit at the price of a greatly increased risk of shipwreck.

The practicalities of these modes of transportation have been tested more than once and the routes seem feasible, but proof is lacking, and none of the reports of bluestones abandoned along the way have been substantiated. Furthermore, much of the discussion of likely routes has been based on archaeological research undertaken in the 1950s. Since then isotopic work by Sheffield University suggests that cattle were being driven from Wales to Wiltshire by this period. If these animals were going in this direction anyway, it would be surprising if it had not occurred to people to use them as beasts of burden; a relatively uncomplaining mode of transport for the stones which they could have dragged on sleds.

With cattle to take the effort of haulage, and rafts to assist on water courses, a greater issue than the labour involved would have been the negotiation of a route through the various territories along the way. Even in medieval times, a journey from Pembrokeshire to Wiltshire involved passage through the lands of several rulers, and there seems no reason to believe that the situation was much different in earlier times. This was a feat of political as well as physical effort.

And then there is the even greater question of why the project should have been undertaken at all. Certainly the transportation of so many large stones across such a great distance is unique in the prehistory of Britain and Ireland, but there is some evidence from other regions for the pursuit of specific types of stone in construction projects. For example research by Mark Patton has shown that in Jersey large stones were sometimes transported several kilometres to be used in the construction of tombs; and at both Newgrange and Knowth in Ireland, the mounds of passage tombs were embellished with cobbles brought from several locations, some over 40km away. Although these stones were much smaller and more manageable than those used at Stonehenge, this loose parallel from Ireland is of particular interest, since Stonehenge also demonstrates the collection of stones from varied distant sources – the Preseli Hills and elsewhere in south Wales. This gifting of stones, and their unification at a distant site, may have been a way of demonstrating allegiances, and of binding the community around Stonehenge into a much wider social network. The effect may have been similar, albeit on a grossly exaggerated scale, to that which had been perpetuated through the exchange of stone axes for more than a millennium.

2400 BC and after. Bowing to the habits of foreigners

State of the nation

In imagining the period covered by this book it is easy to see a dance of monuments and artefacts, shifting and changing through different forms and locations. Harder to visualise is the landscape in which these events took place.

The basic shape of the country was much the same as it is today. Millennia of sea level rise had nearly reached an equilibrium with the land, bringing the shoreline close to its present position. The broad topography was also the same – the mountains have not moved, nor have the hills and valleys. But there were considerable differences in the detail of the country's landscape. Some basic landscape features were not yet established including the great sand dunes now found along the coasts of Glamorgan, Gower, Pembrokeshire and Anglesey. In other areas, such as at Porth Neigwl on the Llyn peninsula, a fertile plain which once extended far into the Irish Sea has since been eaten away by thousands of tides, leaving only the curve of a beach and a seascape.

Inland, many of the rivers meandered in different channels from those they occupy today; and the land beside them was different too. Since this period a depth of over 4.5m of silt has been washed into Llyn Geirionydd which sits above the Conwy Valley and almost 6m have been deposited in parts of Llangorse Lake near Brecon, all washed from hills which were once covered in thick rich soils, but are now relatively impoverished, and all a consequence of more recent ploughing and loss of trees.

At this time Wales was still more wooded than not, with a canopy that rose up to the higher slopes of the mountains. People had been forcing clearings in it for millennia, and doubtless there were some more fertile areas where the woods had been reduced to small islands amidst grassland. For the most part each of these clearings had been abandoned after a time, leaving the trees to return if the quality of the soils still allowed it and if grazing did not prevent it. The long views across the landscape, so easily taken for granted today, were still a rarity. Away from the

Location of sites in Wales
mentioned in this chapter.

1 Banc Tynddol
2 Bedd Branwen
3 Bodtegir
4 Brymbo
5 Capel Eithin
6 Capel Garmon
7 Castell Coch
8 Clynnog
9 Coed y Dinas
10 Collfryn
11 Copa Hill
12 Crawcwellt West
13 Cwm Car
14 Cwm Du
15 Dolfrwynog
16 Dyffryn Ardudwy
17 Erglodd
18 Fairy Mount
19 Four Crosses
20 Graig Lwyd
21 Hendre
22 Llancaiach-isaf
23 Llandderfel
24 Llandegai
25 Llangorse Lake
26 Llanharry
27 Llanllyfni
28 Llannon
29 Llithfaen
30 Llyn Geirionydd
31 Ludchurch
32 Merthyr Mawr
33 Meusydd
34 Moel Arthur
35 Moel Hebog
36 Nab Head
37 Newborough Warren
38 Pant-y-Saer
39 Paviland
40 Penderyn
41 Penywyrlod, Llanigon
42 Plas Heaton
43 Pontrhydygroes
44 Porth Neigwl
45 Pyle
46 Riley's Tumulus
47 South Hill, Talbenny
48 St Fagans
49 Sutton 268'
50 Thornwell Farm
51 Tinkinswood
52 Tonfannau Quarry
53 Twyn Bryn Glas
54 Ty Newydd
55 Ty-Isaf
56 Tyn-y-fron
57 Usk
58 Vaynor Farm
59 Welsh St Donats
60 Ysgwennant

© The National Museum of
Wales (Jackie Chadwick,
Tony Daly).

54   2400 BC and after

settlements, these woods were home to many animals now extinct in Wales, such as eagles, wild cattle, brown bear, wolves, beavers and wildcats. Other animals which survive today would have been more common: red deer, roe deer and wild boar to name a few. In the wildwoods a walker would have felt safer with a bow, a knife, and a dog.

This was the Wales of 2400 BC, a backdrop to a series of innovations which were to transform the lives of those who lived here.

Red gold from the west

In August 1920, Evans Hoyle, Director of the National Museum of Wales, received word that Mrs Winifred T Wynne of Peniarth was preparing to donate her father-in-law's collection of antiquities. William Watkin Edward Wynne had been a renowned antiquarian, amassing an important group of Welsh manuscripts and an outstanding range of archaeological finds. So, on offer was a chance to preserve one of the nation's finest privately owned collections and Evans Hoyle resolved not to miss it. Within a few months, the necessary formalities had been resolved and the artefacts were being prepared for exhibition by the Head of Archaeology, Mortimer Wheeler. In the collection was a flat metal axe, much pitted with corrosion and fractured across the middle. Wheeler notes that many items in the Wynne of Peniarth collection had lost their labels, and it seems likely that the axe was one of them since he could only record that it had probably been found in Merionethshire (now southern Gwynedd), in keeping with much of the rest of the collection. Even

The Merionethshire axe, one of the earliest copper artefacts known from Wales. Formerly in William Watkin Edward Wynne's collection of antiquities, most of which came from southern Gwynedd.

© The National Museum of Wales (Kevin Thomas).

Original artefact housed in the collections of Amgueddfa Cymru – National Museum Wales (15.4cm long).

so, the axe was interesting because its simple form – just a metal slab with a slight widening at the blade end – suggested to Wheeler that it was one of the earliest examples of metalworking to have been found in Wales.

Three years later, Wheeler sent the axe to be analysed by Cecil Henry Desch of Sheffield University, a metallurgist with a strong interest in history. He found it was made of copper, albeit with significant impurities. Desch was principally interested in the presence of nickel among these, and he suggested that the copper ore might have come from the Rhuddlan area of Denbighshire. But, with the benefit of more recent work, including a resampling of the axe by Peter Northover of Oxford University, it can now be seen that the high levels of antimony and arsenic which Desch also noticed are more useful in revealing the axe's origins.

The focus on these elements stems from a programme of work begun in 1952 by a committee of the Royal Anthropological Institute which aimed to source the metals used in early British and Irish tools. After five years of work they reported on the result of almost a hundred metallurgical analyses of copper and bronze tools, with sixty-four tools showing broadly the same impurity pattern to those of the Merionethshire axe. Herbert H Coghlan and Humphrey Case sought a match for this pattern among ores from across Britain and Ireland and found one in those from Co Kerry in southwest Ireland. Furthermore, of sixteen copper axes sharing the same early form as the Merionethshire example, all but one was made of metal of this type. Here was evidence that Co Kerry had been a major supplier at the dawn of metalworking in Ireland, and the Merionethshire axe demonstrated that its products had reached Wales.

Over the years, further analyses have confirmed a link between early metalwork found in Wales and the rest of Britain, and an ore source from southwest Ireland. But the real breakthrough in the sourcing of the Merionethshire axe and other similar specimens came as a result of fieldwork begun in 1992 by William O'Brien then of the National University of Ireland, Galway. His work identified a mine and an adjacent settlement set on a peninsula known as Ross Island, jutting into Lough Leane near Killarney. The settlement had been occupied between about 2400 and 1900 BC and consisted of simple huts, the debris of daily life, crushed rock from the mine, stone hammers, furnace pits, droplets of copper, and an ingot.

The people of Ross Island had probably been attracted to the stains of copper minerals exposed in a 300m stretch of limestone along the edge of the lake. They had collected this ore by setting fires against the surrounding limestone to weaken it and had then hammered off fragments which they sorted to remove larger pieces of limestone. Copper-rich pieces were then taken to the nearby settlement and

shoreline for further grinding and smelting. Chemical and lead isotope analysis of the copper they left behind, as well as experimental work on ore from the mine has shown it to be a good match for the arsenic-rich copper used to make the Merionethshire axe. It seems the source of some of the earliest metalwork yet discovered in Britain and Ireland has been found.

The first metal tools

The concentration of early copper tools in Ireland and their apparent link to Ross Island are striking. O'Brien has calculated that if a tonne of copper was produced each year, this could have been cast to make over 2,000 axes of average weight. Within a century, even allowing for losses, thousands of copper tools would have been in circulation, easily enough to allow some to be carried to Britain soon after production began.

For those who could obtain one of these axes, there were considerable practical benefits to be had. A woodsman who carried a copper axe had to hand a more versatile tool than a man who held a stone axe. The blade was thinner and sharper,

The Moel Arthur Hoard (Flintshire).

These three axes of early design were found eroding from a hillside where they had presumably been buried as a group.

© The National Museum of Wales (Steve Burrow).

Original artefacts housed in the collections of Manchester Museum. (Each axe is around 16.5cm long).

so trees could be felled more speedily and wood could be worked with greater refinement. A blunted or damaged copper blade could also be resharpened more rapidly than a stone one, and a broken copper axe could be recast to make a new one. Functional benefit aside, the simple status that could be gathered by owning one of these gleaming red-gold blades may have been a major motivating factor in their acquisition. But polished stone axes had served their purpose for over a thousand years and the initial rarity of copper meant they could not all have been abandoned overnight. Furthermore, the ready availability of suitable stone probably meant it was easier for some people to continue making and using stone axes, rather than investing effort in forging links with metal-rich communities in Ireland. Having said that, there is no conclusive evidence for continued axe production at the major workshops in southwest Wales or at Graig Lwyd and it is possible that any continued manufacture of stone axes after this time was undertaken in a more ad hoc manner.

While copper axes mirrored a long-established stone tool type, smiths were also experimenting with new uses for their material. One result was the halberd, an ungainly and threatening object, which has no precedent in stone. The halberd is a long dagger-like blade, mounted roughly at right angles to a haft and designed for piercing and cutting. They were used across Europe, with a notable concentration in Ireland; indeed it has been argued that they may have originated here, shortly after the first adoption of metallurgy.

Copper halberd from Dolfrwynog (Gwynedd).

The blade of this, and other, halberds demonstrates considerable sophistication on the part of the smith. A central rib provides strength to the piece, which is fixed to the haft with rivets. These rivets are often made of a softer metal than the blade, making them easier to hammer into place. Carvings in the foothills of the Alps show halberd blades mounted on short hafts like tomahawks, and also on long pike-like poles.

Several halberds made from Irish copper have been found in Wales, including one near a later mine at Pontrhydygroes in Ceredigion, and two discovered during quarrying at Tonfannau Quarry in Gwynedd.

© The National Museum of Wales.

Original artefact housed in the collections of Amgueddfa Cymru – National Museum of Wales. (Length 29.5cm).

Fighting with halberds.

It has been suggested that halberds were used in staged combats, being too cumbersome for pitched battles.

© The National Museum of Wales (Tony Daly).

There has been much debate about the function of halberds largely on account of their apparent awkwardness – an angled blade set on a long pole could be deflected with relative ease, allowing a defender under their attacker's guard; the long blade would also prove quite fragile if used against a hard target. A detailed study of Irish halberds by Ronan O'Flaherty has shown that these sometimes have damage around the rivets, as though from impact forcing the blade back in to the handle. Twisting of the blade in the grip may also have been an issue – some metal-shafted examples from Europe have an oval cross-section, presumably to prevent this.

This unwieldiness suggests that the halberd was a weapon which was only effective against an opponent fighting with a similar weapon, or no weapon at all. This may imply a role in single combat or perhaps in ritualised battles. O'Flaherty draws parallels with the use of medieval halberds to suggest that under such conditions the handle may have been used for the attack, like a quarterstaff while the blade delivered the killing blow.

It is interesting that this first metal should have been used for such masculine ends – the creation of axes and halberds – and to this list can be added the making of daggers also – but copper was not reserved exclusively for such items. Thin slivers were also used to make awls which were in turn used to pierce leather or other soft materials, these were functions which evidence from excavated burials would suggest were more normally associated with women at this time than men. Even so, it is notable that 'male' goods consumed far more of this presumably rare material than did goods more likely to be linked to women.

Exploring the land of plenty

Living in a modern metal age it seems obvious that people in Wales should have grasped the potential of Irish copper when it first became available and sought similar resources in their own land. Certainly there were plenty to be had.

The mountainous parts of Wales are rich in minerals deposited hundreds of millions of years ago. In central Wales, hot mineral-rich fluids left veins of copper, lead, zinc and gold, as they permeated through fractures and faults in the surrounding rocks. Subsequent mountain building and erosion brought these veins closer to the surface. On Anglesey, gases and solutions, driven by submarine volcanic springs, permeated rock to create massive ore bodies; and in northeast Wales waters carried minerals upwards through limestone until they met impermeable rocks and were precipitated out of solution. In 2400 BC, the country would have been virgin territory for prospectors and many surface sources must have been present which have since been removed.

There are some hints that prospectors explored Wales's mountains within a few centuries of Irish copper being introduced to this country, although counter-arguments can be made in each case. At Copa Hill, in Ceredigion, an exposed copper vein was quarried at some point before 2000 BC, and the excavator Simon Timberlake has suggested that the exploitation of this site's copper ore as a pigment may date back much further. At Erglodd, on the edge of Borth Bog in Ceredigion, fire-setting and ore-crushing was probably underway before 2100 BC, and this could have been the work of some of Wales's earliest metallurgists, although again it is possible, that these miners might have been searching for lead and perhaps copper to use as a pigment. Some mining may also have taken place before 2000 BC at Tyn-y-fron in the Rheidol Valley, Ceredigion. Across the border, in Cheshire, charcoal found in spoil from a copper mine at Alderley Edge dates to around 2400 BC, although this is not conclusive proof of mining, since the charcoal may be much older than

the mining activity – which was certainly in progress by 1900 BC – and may have been incorporated into the spoil by chance.

The discovery of these ore sources (whenever it occurred) would have required a detailed knowledge of the land, suggesting the involvement of local people. Several sixteenth- and seventeenth-century accounts illustrate how they might have identified ore sources. In a work of 1653, Gabriel Plattes records that minerals occur in 'rocky and craggy mountaynes ... the more barren they are, the greater prob-ability there is that they containe rich Mines and Minerals.' And indeed, veins of minerals are more likely to be found at changes in topography, which in turn mark faults through which minerals may

Thrift (Armeria maritima) growing on old mine spoil in Snowdonia.

Some plants, like this one, have a particular tolerance to copper-rich soils making their presence significant in the identification of potential sources of ore.

© The National Museum of Wales (Tim Rich).

have penetrated the rocks. For a prospector, the landscape of Wales provided many such places to explore. John Webster, in 1671, recommended that streams in likely areas should be examined for fragments of ore which would be distinguishable by their weight and colour. These could then be traced back to an eroding source. Once a likely area had been located, changes in vegetation were also good indicators of the presence of minerals.

Analysis of a copper axe from Llandderfel in Gwynedd by Peter Northover suggests that copper from North Wales was being used before 2200 BC, but the dominance of Irish metal in the objects which have been analysed suggest that such enterprises were not on a large scale. A number of reasons can be proposed for the slow start in the development of ore extraction in Wales. The prestige to be had in being part of an Irish exchange network may have been greater than the credit to be gained

Two halberds and a fragment from a dagger, found at Castell Coch just north of Cardiff.

Analysis by Stuart Needham and Brenda Rohl of the lead isotopes in these artefacts suggests that they were made from copper from either southwest Britain, or possibly even further afield in northwest Europe.

© The National Museum of Wales.

Original artefacts housed in the collections of Amgueddfa Cymru – National Museum of Wales. (Longest halberd 26.4cm).

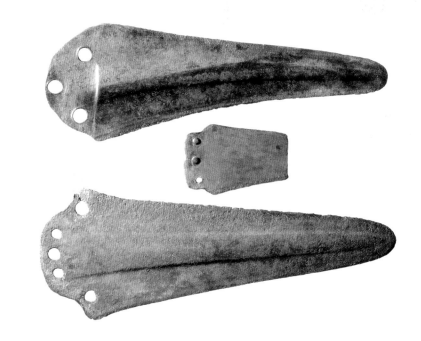

Several types of copper ore are found in Britain and Ireland.

The greens and golds of Wales's malachite (front) and chalcopyrite (back left) may have been overlooked by prospectors who were more familiar with the grey arsenic-rich tennantite (back right) found in southwest Ireland.

© The National Museum of Wales (Kevin Thomas).

Original specimens housed in the collections of Amgueddfa Cymru – National Museum of Wales.

from exploiting a local ore source. It is also possible that the skill of transforming ore into copper was a guarded secret, surrounded by cultural taboos as to who could perform this magic. If this was the case, people in Wales may not have linked the gleaming copper axes made in Ireland with the coloured veins of rock in their own land. Once Wales's ores had been recognised the copper which could be produced from them would also have made slightly softer tools than the arsenic-hardened ones the metalworkers of Ross Island were able to produce. There may therefore have been a perception that local resources were inferior, delaying their widespread use.

Whether one, all, or none of these reasons applied, it was to be several centuries before copper from Wales made a significant contribution to the quantity of metal in circulation in Britain and it is possible that people were similarly slow in recognising the potential of another mineral known to have been exploited across Britain and Ireland from about this time: gold.

At the time of writing a kilogram of gold cost many thousands of pounds, while the same amount of copper and scrap iron cost just a few pounds and pence respectively. Such figures leave little room for doubt about the high cultural value which the modern world ascribes to this material, but people have not always treated it in this way. If one looks back across the tens of millennia of human history, gleaming gold seems to have been ignored until relatively recently, despite being far easier to recognise than other metals which must be won from their ores.

Setting aside its perceived beauty, it is possible that part of this delay was due to gold's softness, a property which limits the range of uses to which it can be put. Before gold could become an object of desire there had to be an acceptance that it had more potential than its mechanical properties would suggest. If objects were to be made which were larger than an individual nugget, then the ability to control high temperature fires was also needed. These cultural and technological hurdles seem to have been crossed in Europe by around 4500 BC, notably at Varna in Bulgaria where almost 300 people were buried, some accompanied by a total of 3,000 pieces of gold jewellery and ornament. In Wales the leap came later.

Objects which were aesthetically pleasing rather than functionally necessary had been used in Wales since human occupation began: ivory ornaments and perforated sea-shells accompanied the 29,000 year old 'Red Lady' of Paviland found on Gower, the first burial of a modern human in Wales; strings of stone beads were made at Nab Head in Pembrokeshire around 8400 BC. But such items remained very rare: just three beads have been found in Wales from the entire fifteen centuries spanning 4000 until 2500 BC.

To date, the earliest evidence for the wearing of gold ornament in Wales comes from close to the Copa Hill mine site at Banc Tynddol in Ceredigion, where Simon Timberlake discovered a disc, about the size of a milk bottle top and weighing just 2.5 grams, during the excavation of a Roman and early medieval smelting site. Subsequent excavation suggests the disc came from a shallow grave which may once have been covered by a cairn. It was probably made from alluvial gold and had been hammered and polished flat, before dots and concentric circles were impressed onto its surface. At its centre were two holes, suggesting that it had once been threaded to a garment. Similar gold ornaments, of which about thirty are known from Britain and Ireland, date from about 2400 BC.

One other item of goldwork from Wales may be of a similarly early date. A crescent-shaped necklace found at Llanllyfni in Gwynedd, but since the form of this necklace is similar to that of other necklaces worn after 2200 BC it is discussed in the next chapter.

Almost certainly, many more trinkets of gold were worn by people in Wales at this time, but the ease with which gold can be worked meant that a worn or damaged ornament could be melted and hammered to make a new one, rather than being thrown away. As a result, incorruptible gold may have been recycled for many generations, leaving little for archaeologists to find. The ease with which this can happen is well illustrated by an analysis undertaken by the Irish archaeologist George Eogan. He observed that in the past Irish jewellers bought up ancient gold artefacts and melted them down to make saleable forms. In total he estimated that at least a thousand items were lost to this trade in the first half of the nineteenth-century alone, and with this in mind it is not difficult to appreciate the vast number of items that may have been lost over the past 4,000 years.

Continental designs

The first metallurgists at Ross Island in Ireland were users of Beakers – the style of pottery which had become almost ubiquitous in western Europe by this time. The appearance of metalwork and the adoption of Beakers probably coincided in Wales as well, but whereas in Ireland Beakers are generally found on settlement or ritual sites, in Wales they are more often found with burials. This suggests that the two sides of the Irish Sea drew their influences from different parts of Europe. Ireland's use of Beakers seems to be linked most strongly to traditions current along the Atlantic coast of France and Spain. While Wales was more influenced by trends in the rest of Britain and northern Europe.

Poor preservation of bone in Wales, and the vagaries of early excavators, mean that few secure radiocarbon dates have been obtained from those buried with Beakers, but there are a few vessels which can be dated on stylistic grounds to the earliest use of this pottery in Britain. These are generally decorated all over with impressions made by bands of twisted cord or comb. Sherds from pots like these have been found on Anglesey, at Newborough Warren where they were discovered eroding from sand dunes, and fragments have also been found in ancient tombs at Tinkinswood and Thornwell Farm in south Wales. But there is no evidence that the users of Beakers in Wales built tombs themselves.

The question of invasion

Beakers are an anomaly in Wales. After so many generations in which people in Britain seem to have been content to build on the heritage of their forefathers, both in monument and artefact styles, here suddenly was a European pottery style. Until the 1970s the explanation for their appearance was clear; they were the debris dropped by continental migrants: therefore Beakers represented a replacement of an old population with fresh blood. Given the impact of other episodes of migration on British history – Saxon, Viking, Irish and Norman – it is not surprising that large

numbers of researchers accepted the logic of this argument and were drawn to the study of this earlier period.

Support for the migration theory also seemed to come from the bodies that were found with Beakers. Throughout the nineteenth-century there was agreement that they were of a different racial type from those who had come before. The people buried in tombs around 3600 BC had long narrow skulls, while those buried around 2400 BC had broad short skulls. In 1912, John Abercromby, the father of Beaker studies in Britain, summarised this racial type as follows:

the general aspect of [their faces were] rugged and forbidding [...] The cheekbones were prominent and the nose projected much beyond the prominent eyebrows; the lower jaw was square, massive [...] Coupled with teeth often of extraordinary size many of these invaders must have presented the appearance of great ferocity and brutality, in a degree which far surpasses our modern conventional representation of the criminal of the type of Bill Sikes.

He estimated that up to 600 of these savage-looking folk had landed on the shores of Britain, breeding and spreading rapidly until they were present in their thousands across the country.

In Wales, as elsewhere, it became common to characterise broad and rugged-skulled individuals from this time as 'Beaker-folk'; skeletons buried at St Fagans in Glamorgan, Riley's Tumulus in Bridgend, Llanharry in Rhondda Cynon Taf, and Brymbo in Wrexham have all been described in this manner. Indeed, the skull from Brymbo has been reconstructed by forensic anthropologist Caroline Wilkinson and the facial type described by Abercromby can be clearly seen. But in the early 1990s Neil Brodie studied afresh the skulls of this period and his work suggests that the shape of the skull cannot answer the question of whether Wales was invaded at this time. Brodie argues that if the appearance of this broad skull shape in Britain was the result of a migration around 2400 BC then it should not be found before

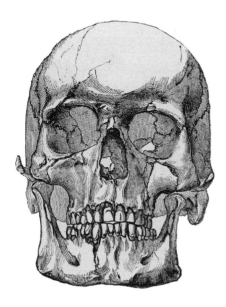 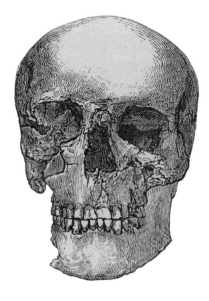

Skulls of two middle-aged men recorded by nineteenth-century physiologist George Rolleston and published in William Greenwell's British Barrows. The example on the left typifies the broad-type commonly associated with this period, the long-type on the right is often thought to be typical of an earlier population. The reality is probably more complex than this.

© The National Museum of Wales (Tony Daly).

Forensic reconstruction of a man buried at Brymbo (Wrexham). He was interred with a Beaker.

© The National Museum of Wales (Steve Burrow).

Original artefacts and reconstruction housed in the collections of Wrexham County Borough Museum.

this time. But his measurement of almost 250 skulls suggested that in fact, the shape of peoples' heads had been gradually changing before this date, from long-narrow to broad-rugged, perhaps in response to a changing climate, or a change in behaviour.

More recently, an alternative line of evidence has breathed fresh life into the debate. At present results are only available from a few analyses, but one very striking study is worth highlighting. Around 2300 BC, about 5km southeast of Stonehenge, a 35 to 45 year old man was buried with great wealth, including Beakers, gold and copper objects and archery equipment, hence his popular name 'The Amesbury Archer'. Isotopic analysis of his teeth suggest that he was raised in the Alps. Is this evidence of a successful migration from the continent, or of a lone traveller?

A subsequent discovery, at Boscombe Down, also near Stonehenge, raises the number of potential migrants a little higher. Here, around the same time, the remains of seven people of different ages were buried in a single grave. The strontium isotope signatures of three of them hint that they were brought up in an area of palaeo-zoic rocks, with the most likely area on archaeological grounds being Brittany, although on geo-logical grounds alone it is possible that they came from elsewhere in Europe, or perhaps more locally, from western Britain. All three moved from their birthplace dur-ing adolescence, and then moved again to die near Stonehenge. Furthermore, each had set off on their travels when they were the same age, but in different years, suggesting there was a tradition of sending adolescents on a migratory route that led them to this area.

The Amesbury Archer and Bos-combe Bowmen lend support

The grave of the Amesbury Archer (Wiltshire).
© Wessex Archaeology.

to the idea of a migration into Britain at this time, but without more evidence for foreigners within Wales itself it is impossible to say whether this movement of people reached as far as this region. Wales's later history of resistance to Roman and Saxon incursions would suggest the need for a cautious view.

Whatever the case, those travellers who entered Wales would have found themselves to be a minority in a well-populated country. It would have been the local population who decided whether the newcomers' ways were to prosper. Some may have adopted the new styles of artefacts – both pottery and metal – along with the continental burial rite as a means of standing out among their peers, others may have resisted the changing times and sought comfort in tradition. Britain was as complicated then as it is now. In Wales, the evidence fits this mixed picture of continuity and change, suggesting a people sifting through the cultural traditions of their land, maintaining or adapting some and discarding others in the face of fresh opportunities.

Out with the old

Among the ancient traditions to decline were well-known forms of flint artefacts, including the large discoidal knives and some types of arrowheads. Archaeologists have focused most attention on the apparent abandonment of Grooved Ware pots. In Wales there is little evidence for the continued use of this pottery after 2300 BC, with some of the latest sites where the pottery style was used including Capel Eithin on Anglesey and Hendre in Flintshire. But while the Grooved Ware style was itself abandoned, the users of Beakers continued the earlier tradition of burying their pottery in pits. For example at Collfryn in northern Powys, broken Beakers were buried in a long, shallow pit around 2200 BC, at Crawcwellt West in Gwynedd the same kind of activity took place around 2100 BC, and within the Llandegai henge around 2000 BC. Broken Beakers were also buried in other less well-dated pits at Bedd Branwen on Anglesey, Four Crosses in northern Powys, and just across the Welsh border at Bromfield near Ludlow in Shropshire.

While it can be seen that both Grooved Ware and Beakers were used in activities which entailed the burial of broken pottery, it is likely that these activities were quite different. It has been suggested that Grooved Ware pots were used as cooking vessels, with smaller examples probably being used for serving. In contrast, and as their name suggests the tall sinuous profile of many Beakers has suggested a drinking cup in the minds of archaeologists. Indeed, several later examples have

single handles, reinforcing this association, for example Beakers from Cwm Du in southern Powys and Twyn Bryn Glas in Rhondda Cynon Taf.

Studies of well-preserved Beakers – generally those found in graves – show that most were of a size well-suited to this function, with those found in Wales normally being large enough to hold a good-sized drink, although outsize examples are known from elsewhere. But if most Beakers were well-suited to holding liquid the question to be asked is what liquid? For some time the assumption has been that Beakers were linked to the drinking of alcohol or other inebriating concoctions. This view is based on the discovery of residues, possibly of mead, in Beakers found in Scotland, and on the discovery of psychotropic alkaloids and traces of beer in pots from Spain. Whether Beakers were adopted in Wales because of their links to beer-soaked rituals is a speculation never likely to be proven without fresh finds since Beakers found by early excavators tended to be well-cleaned upon discovery. For example, the Beaker from Llanharry in Glamorgan, was said to have been filled with 'slimy stuff' until it was plunged into a bucket of water by the finder. But it is interesting to note that there are three sites in Wales where Beakers have been found associated with barley grains, a primary ingredient of beer. At Moel Hebog in Gwynedd, grains had become stuck to the outside of a Beaker before it was fired, at Coed y Dinas 1 in northern Powys, barley grains were found in a patch of charcoal associated with Beaker pottery, and at Four Crosses 2, twelve kilometres to the north, a pit was found which contained both Beakers and grains of barley. These cases demonstrate that the users of Beakers grew barley, whether they malted that barley to make beer remains to be confirmed.

Ancient monuments

Not all was change at this time, and there is some evidence for continuity in the years before and after 2400 BC. The reuse of megalithic tombs has already been noted, but henge monuments also continued to be built and used.

People had been digging pits at the Llandegai henge since about 2800 BC, and this practice continued for centuries after 2400 BC. Around 2300 BC a pit was dug and within it were placed a small plank and piece of flint; around two centuries later two more were dug. In one was buried a burnt wooden tray covered in pebbles; in the other, at the centre of the henge, cremated remains were buried, packed around with stones. Then, about 2000 BC a fourth pit was dug and a Beaker pot and another wooden tray were buried within it. The pot was already well-used and may have been broken when it was buried. But the most striking evidence for an

Pit outside the entrance of the Llandegai henge (Gwynedd).

This large pit was originally shored with wood, large stones filled the gaps between the shoring and the pit's edge. The area within this was swept clean before the cremated bones of a single individual were set on its base.

© The National Museum of Wales.

appreciation of earlier ritual practices at Llandegai comes from a very large pit dug just 8m beyond the southwest entrance of the henge. Its position mirrored very closely that of the circle of pits which had been dug outside the entrance of the adjacent enclosure, Llandegai A, some 700 years earlier. It is unlikely that this was coincidental. Furthermore, this new pit also mirrored the old in holding cremated bone. Anyone entering the henge would have been forced to walk over, or around, this burial place, just as the people of 3000 BC had walked over or around burials in their earlier enclosure.

Evidence for the adoption of henges by Beaker users can also be seen at Vaynor Farm in Carmarthenshire where work in advance of a gas pipeline revealed sherds of Beakers in the ditch of another henge, demonstrating its use after 2400 BC. Of equal interest here is the henge at Dyffryn Lane, in northern Powys, which radiocarbon dates suggest was probably built around an earlier stone circle sometime after 2500 BC.

In combination the evidence suggests that henges continued to be valued after some communities in Wales had adopted Beakers – a trend evident at many sites elsewhere in Britain.

Dyffryn Lane henge (northern Powys) under excavation by Alex Gibson (Bradford University) in 2006.

© Crown copyright (Royal Commission on the Ancient and Historical Monuments of Wales).

The honoured dead

Much has been made of the near total absence of burials before 2400 BC – a few ghosted or burnt skeletons for 600 years of living – but after this time the placing of the dead in the earth became far more common.

In some cases, the manner of burial is very similar to that demonstrated by the sparse evidence from previous centuries, the cremated remains at Llandegai for example, or the re-use of megalithic tombs, but the most obvious burial rite from this time is one without clear precedent in Wales: the inhumation of the dead, crouched as though asleep, often alone and accompanied by a Beaker. The continental fashion for burying an individual with grave goods had arrived.

This form of burial continued to be used for around six hundred years. Differences of detail are apparent in some later examples – for example, in the manner in which the grave was marked, and in the quantity of grave goods deposited. In a few cases radiocarbon dates confirm that a specific burial is late in the history of this rite, but for many of the simpler Beaker graves it is very difficult to know exactly when the burial took place. For this reason what follows is an overview of the Beaker burial rite in Wales as a whole, separating out for comment in the next chapter only those sites which are known to be late in the history of this type of burial.

Plan of Beaker burial found at Llithfaen (Gwynedd) in 1937.

This cist had been covered by a road surface and was discovered by workmen digging through it to lay a pipe.

© Cambrian Archaeological Association.

The form of the burial

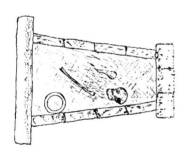

Discoveries at Llithfaen in Gwynedd illustrates the Beaker burial rite well. Here a pit was dug and lined with stone slabs to form a cist. Into this was lain the body of a man, set in a crouched position and with a Beaker at his feet. A capstone sealed his resting place. For the mourners this burial rite involved considerable labour: stone slabs had to be sourced and dragged to the right spot, a pit had to be dug to receive them, sometimes through soft earth; sometimes, as at Ludchurch in Pembrokeshire, a cist was cut into solid rock. Not surprisingly, some mourners chose a simpler route. At the, probably later, Beaker sites of Riley's Tumulus in Bridgend and South Hill, Talbenny in Pembrokeshire, bodies and their Beakers were buried in simple dug graves.

It has been argued that these burials represent a new trend in society reflecting the rise of powerful individuals, but this hypothesis does not seem wholly convincing. Powerful people

Cist at Clynnog (Gwynedd) with its capstone removed to reveal a Beaker inside.

A local doctor analysed bones from this cist and pronounced that they belonged to a child although, since the doctor also allowed the possibility that they were the remains of a dog, his competency in this area is open to question.

The presence of a low mound over this cist suggests that it may have been built some time after the introduction of Beakers into Wales.

© Cambrian Archaeological Association.

had been present long before 2400 BC – the great works in the Walton Basin and in coordinating the movement of Stonehenge's bluestones are evidence of their presence. Furthermore, the fact that a small part of the population was honoured in death after 2400 BC is not proof that these were the most powerful people in life. The criteria for their selection are unknown, as are the fates of the many thousands of other people who died in this period.

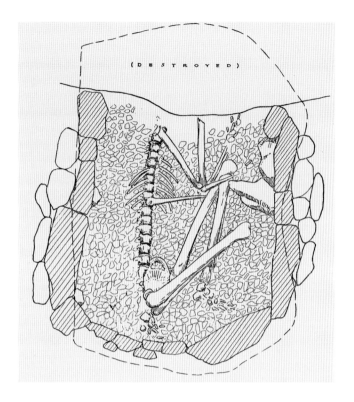

The grave and its occupant

For the most part these cists are of a size appropriate to the burial of a single crouched adult body, but some much larger cists are known. For example, a 1.5 by 0.9m cist at Llannon in Carmarthenshire, could easily have held two people; indeed the covering slab was so large that it was carted away and used to cap a vault in the nearby cemetery of Llwyn-teg. But the absence of surviving human remains from this and other large cists makes it impossible to decide whether they were made large in order to receive more than one body or whether they were made to give more room for a single individual. In other instances the evidence is clearer and multiple burial in a single cist can certainly be demonstrated, as at St Fagans in Glamorgan, where a 1.35m square capstone covered a cist which held the remains of two bodies, one old and one young, and at Ludchurch in Pembrokeshire where parts of four people were found together. Radiocarbon dates have also revealed three burials for the period from 2400 until about 2200 BC in the chambered tomb at Thornwell Farm near Chepstow. Clearly there was no fundamental requirement for the dead to be buried alone.

At the other extreme, cists too small to hold an adult body are also known, for example at Bodtegir in Conwy, and Twyn Bryn Glas in Rhondda Cynon Taf. The excavator of Twyn Bryn Glas, Derek Webley, suggested that bulky bodies might have been placed in these unexpectedly small spaces by binding their limbs, although he allowed for other explanations, most obviously that small cists were designed for small people, presumably children. Certainly children were honoured in Beaker cist burials, for example at Llancaiach-isaf in Caerphilly where a three-year-old child afflicted with rickets was buried.

Young and old, men and women, the current evidence suggests that all were eligible for burial in a cist, although in Wales adult men have been identified most frequently. In some parts of Britain it has been recognised that men were afforded a different burial rite than women, often being found interred on their left side, with women lying on their right. It is not known how widespread this variation was in Wales, but the only female burial for which accurate information exists, Welsh St Donats 3 in Glamorgan, conforms to this pattern, as do the men buried at Sutton 268', nine kilometres to the west, and Brymbo in Wrexham. The only burial of a man which bucks this trend is that found at Llithfaen.

Property of the dead

In contrast to the many and varied items which accompanied the Amesbury Archer, people in Wales seemed to have been buried modestly in this period – most of the country's richer Beaker burials can be argued to be later on grounds of radiocarbon date or associated burial ritual. A few flints are all that is normally found, as at Llannon in Carmarthenshire, or an arrowhead, as at Cwm Car in Merthyr Tydfil. There is also an intriguing account of a small spindle whorl being found with a Beaker at Penderyn in Rhondda Cynon Taf which, if true, gives Wales its earliest evidence for spinning and textile production. But it is the Beaker pot which seems to unite burial rites at this time – providing a drink to ease passage into the afterlife or memorialising a toast made by the mourners – even if the evidence from the St Fagans and Ludchurch burials suggests that the allocation was generally one Beaker per grave, rather than one Beaker per person.

Given that the other major trend of this time was the adoption of metalworking, it is reasonable to wonder why metal objects so rarely accompanied the dead. Indeed, the only metal grave good that can be cited which probably predates 2200 BC is the gold disc from the burial at Banc Tynddol in Ceredigion. With this exception it seems that over these centuries people in Wales did not give valued possessions to their dead, and where possessions were given at all they were the trappings of daily life.

After death

With the ceremonies of death completed and the grave filled in, or capstone replaced, it is likely that many of the first Beaker burials in Wales were only marked with a few stones, a post, or perhaps by local lore. Within a few generations the precise location of many may well have been forgotten. Indeed many cists have only come to light by chance during construction work, as at St Fagans or Brymbo, or when the weight of traffic above them crushed the capstone as happened when a traction engine ran over the cist at Ludchurch. In one case, at Llancaiach-isaf, the cover slab was level with the paving of a farm yard, and its true nature was only discovered by chance by a farm boy.

In contrast, other burial sites were already well-marked, as in the case of the early Beaker burials at megalithic tombs which have already been noted, and to which list could be added other burials, in tombs at Dyffryn Ardudwy in Gwynedd, Penywyrlod (Llanigon) and Ty-Isaf both in southern Powys, Capel Garmon in Conwy, and Pant-y-Saer on Anglesey. Whether the first people to adopt this burial rite ever built monumental mounds of their own is uncertain, although their descendants certainly did so.

The frequency with which bodies are found complete and undisturbed has often led to the view that this was the end of the burial ritual: a person died, was buried, and

Cist at Llancaiach-isaf (Caerphilly).

The capstone had been incorporated into a farmyard's paving.

© The National Museum of Wales.

their resting place was marked; life went on. Not all burials conformed to this pattern. The repeated use of the tomb chamber at Thornwell Farm has already been noted, as have the multiple burials at Ludchurch. At Thornwell it is likely that bodies were simply added to a growing, and long established pile of bones, while at Ludchurch the cist may have been cleared out as completely as possible before the addition of the next body. There is also evidence that not all bodies were placed in their cists intact. At Brymbo the cist contained the partial remains of a single man, with cut-marks to his bones suggesting he had been dismembered after death. The burial

Cist burial in Brymbo (Wrexham).

The deceased was a 173cm tall man who died aged about 35 years old. A scar on his skull suggests he had probably been struck by an arrow – an injury which he survived.

© The National Museum of Wales.

found at Fairy Mount in Wrexham may have been subjected to a similar burial rite; here accounts record a 'heap of much decomposed bones', as though a skeleton was simply gathered up and bundled into the earth. At Llithfaen the absence of the corpse's left side has been assumed to be a result of decay, but the evidence from Brymbo might hint at another reason.

Such examples serve as a reminder that these people had different values and priorities than those held today. The comforting familiarity associated with the image of a body at rest in a grave belies a foreign mindset.

Part 2

2200 – 1500 BC

A perspective from the east

The world of 3000 BC was not a literate one. Writing was in its infancy in the Nile Valley and Near East and unknown elsewhere; few names were recorded and even fewer deeds described. The cradles of civilisation were as trapped in the anonymous shadows as was Wales. In the centuries which followed, hieroglyphics and cuneiform spread steadily and were employed with increasing sophistication in Egypt and Mesopotamia, while life in Wales remained undocumented. Thanks to advances in writing, and the work of scholars who have interpreted them, it is known that the great king Gilgamesh, subject of the world's earliest surviving epic story, lived in the city of Uruk around 2800 BC, when communities were feasting at Upper Ninepence and constructing the henge at Llandegai. Around 2600 BC, when people were transporting stones from southwest Wales to Stonehenge their accomplishments were being mirrored by the pharaoh Djoser who caused the Step Pyramid to be built at Saqqara. And around 2300 BC, Sargon of Agade was uniting the lands from Iran to the Mediterranean under a single cultural umbrella, while in Europe Beakers were being made by long forgotten potters.

So in another part of the world the period 3000 to 2200 BC saw the rise of civilisations which are remembered to this day, their memory captured in writing; a stark contrast with the continued ambiguity of life in Wales, where 'people' and 'communities' have to be our reference rather than personalities. But the written sources available in the Near East provide one fringe benefit for the study of life in Wales; they offer a reminder that even at this distant time, people all over the world shared familiar human concerns. By 2200 BC, Gilgamesh was remembered in Mesopotamia as a hero who struggled against death itself, and writers in Egypt were recording their own fear of old age and of the trials of life – all themes which resonate today, and would no doubt have done so with the many people in Wales who were seeking to honour their own dead at this time.

This insight aside, for the most part the brilliant light offered by the writings of the Near East and Egypt serves to paint darker the shadows in the pre-literate west. After 2200 BC, the nature of these shadows changes. Before, they were caused as much by a lack of evidence as the difficulty in interpreting it, after this date the quantity of archaeological evidence increases enormously and the difficulty is not so much teasing out information, as containing the flood.

Fuels for a new age

In the eighteenth century AD, Wales became the powerhouse of the global copper industry. By 1750 Swansea was producing half of the copper used in Britain, and in 1768, miners at Parys Mountain on Anglesey discovered the 'Great Lode', a mass of ore which was to place the mountain at the heart of the international copper trade. Welsh copper provided the cooking pots for British families, lined the hulls of Royal Navy ships, and produced currency for the African slave trade.

But while magnates ran an industry such as the world had never seen, the miners themselves began to notice that they were not the first to explore Wales's copper-rich mountains.

The first industrial revolution

Nineteenth-century miners on the Great Orme, a promontory on the north Wales coast, repeatedly encountered old tunnels containing bone and stone tools. In October 1849 they struck one working of which the antiquarian William Owen Stanley wrote:

> On the ground were found a number of stone mauls, of various sizes, described as weighing from about 2lb. to 40lb., and rudely fashioned, having been all, as their appearance suggested, used for breaking, pounding, or detaching the ore from the rock... Great quantities of bones of animals were also found, and some of them, as the miners conjectured, had been used for working out the softer parts of the metallic veins.

In the 1930s Oliver Davies followed up these tantalising clues as part of a project commissioned by the British Association. Drawn by a number of old spoil heaps on the south of the Great Orme, he carried out a small scale excavation; but, in the event the most he found were traces of Roman occupation. The real breakthrough in the recognition of the true antiquity of the Great Orme mines came in the 1970s when Duncan James began to explore the complex. Among his discoveries was a spoil heap in a gallery 25m below the surface, and charcoal from this was dated to around 1200 BC; it was the first time that a radiocarbon date had indicated the survival of a Bronze Age mine in Britain. But this was just the beginning. Since this time, over 6.5km of early tunnels have been discovered, some at a depth of 70m

Location of sites in Wales mentioned in this chapter.

1 Aberpennar
2 Acton Park
3 Betws-y-Coed
4 Bryncroes
5 Cadair Idris
6 Caernarfon
7 Candleston
8 Carno
9 Coedana
10 Copa Hill
11 Ffair Rhos
12 Gop
13 Graig Lwyd
14 Great Orme
15 Grondre
16 Hyssington
17 Llanarthney
18 Llancynfelin
19 Llanfachreth
20 Llanfallteg
21 Llanfyrnach
22 Llangollen
23 Llangwyryfon
24 Llanycil
25 Menai Bridge
26 Moelfre Uchaf
27 Nantyrarian
28 Nantyreira
29 New Mills
30 Ogof Wyddon
31 Parys Mountain
32 Pen-trwyn
33 Preseli Hills
34 St George's
35 Staylittle
36 Twll y mwyn

The Great Orme (Conwy).

The early miners may have lived at the base of this hill, on the land now occupied by Llandudno.

The identity of these people remains unknown, but the subject has been brought into sharp focus by Stephen Oppenheimer of Oxford University. His specialism in population genetics has led him to sample the DNA of people across Britain, including eighteen people from Abergele, just 20km along the coast from the Great Orme. These people showed a marked link with early Spanish populations, raising the possibility that the area had been colonised by miners with continental origins who were seeking out new copper sources. It is an appealing hypothesis, and it will be interesting to see whether it holds as more people are added to the DNA database across Wales.

© The National Museum of Wales (Steve Burrow).

below the surface, and a further 8 to 10km of tunnels are still anticipated. The first radiocarbon date has also been followed by many others which have demonstrated that the mine began much earlier.

The green malachite-stained rocks found on the surface at the Great Orme were probably well known for millennia before their potential began to be realised around 1700 BC. Work probably started by tracing surface veins along joints of bedding planes in the limestone. These had softened the rock around them, making it comparatively easy to excavate the seams, and leaving the harder limestone standing proud to form a cross-cutting maze of open air trenches, each one filled with the spoil from the excavation of the next. The softness of the rock meant that the seams could be chiselled or gouged out with bone tools, and over 33,000 complete or fragmentary digging bones have been found, many stained putrescent green by the copper-rich environment in which they have lain. Analysis by Sean Beecroft has shown that cattle provided the majority of bone tools – their ribs and leg bones providing picks, while their shoulder blades served as shovels – bones from pig, sheep and deer were also used, although far less frequently. These animals were presumably killed to supply food, their bones being stockpiled for the next episode of mining. Harder areas of rock were attacked with stone mauls ranging from fist-sized hammers to large cobbles over 20kg in weight. Over 2,400 stone

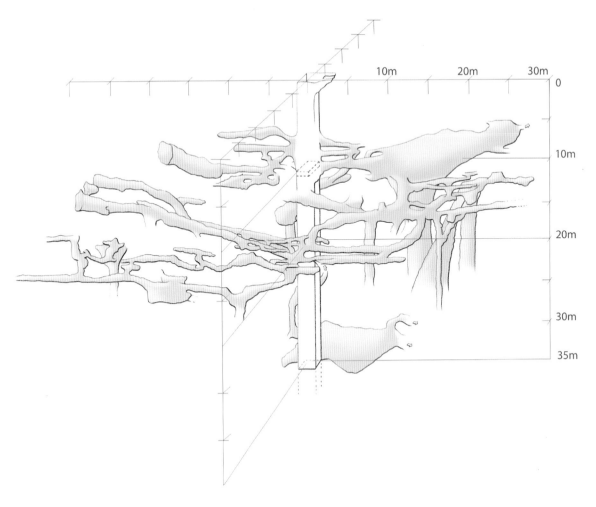

10m

20m

30m

35m

hammers have been recovered from the mines; smaller ones would have been hand-held, bigger ones were probably secured to hafts and swung underarm against the rock face, while the largest of all must have been mounted in cradles where room allowed.

Andrew Lewis suggests that the opencast mine covered an area at least 55m long, by 23m wide and was 8m deep in places; as much as 28,000 tonnes of ore-bearing rock may have been removed from this area. This surface mining was hard physical labour, but it must have seemed easy when compared with the discomfort of working the underground tunnels which were begun towards the end of the period covered by this book.

Simplified plan of the Great Orme mines, as they were known in 1992, shown to a depth of 35m.

The labyrinthine nature of the workings is caused by the meandering and interconnecting veins of malachite each of which was meticulously traced by the miners.

Redrawn by Tony Daly from an original © David Jenkins, Andrew Lewis.

The early tunnels are distinguished from eighteenth- and nineteenth-century mine workings by their rounded sides, and the absence of pick marks and shot holes for explosives. As the miners followed the seams down, they aimed to waste as little time as possible breaking up the worthless rock, and as much time as possible recovering the valuable ore. In some areas this practice led to tunnels so narrow that they could only have been mined by young children; what is more, even small children would have created a bottle-neck in the narrower tunnels, leading to poor ventilation and quickly stifling any open flame. This is the first moment in the history of Wales when the activities of living children can be recognised, and they were not at play or rest, but underground engaged in a task as brutal as that of the Victorian chimneysweep.

More expansive tunnels were dug in areas where the seams were larger or where thoroughfares were needed, the largest areas forming caverns. Like the surface workings, all of this vast network was tunnelled with bone tools and stone mauls, and with fires piled against the rock face to weaken it. This mining technique would have clogged the air with smoke and grime and, if used carelessly, would have suffocated those involved. Even so, if well managed it has been shown to be an effective way of cutting the effort of mining.

Copper ore and stone hammer in one of the tunnels on the Great Orme (Conwy).

Coincidentally, the miners on the Great Orme seem to have preferred hammerstones made of rock tumbled into the sea from the flanks of Graig Lwyd – the same rock which had been used to make axes in previous times. Cobbles of this type can be found along the beaches below the Great Orme, their strength proven by the waves which have rolled them from the foot of Penmaenmawr.

© The National Museum of Wales (Steve Burrow).

Estimates by Andrew Lewis, based on the extent of the tunnels known in the early 1990s, suggest that over 12,600 tonnes of ore-bearing rock was removed from the underground mine, bringing the total, including that from the opencast to over 40,000 tonnes of rock over the centuries that the mine was in use. This figure must now be seen as an underestimate given the many kilometres of additional tunnels which have been identified more recently. While Ross Island could have supplied the comparatively small demand for copper in the early years of metallurgy, the Great Orme was well placed to service the much greater demand which was to follow, and it was by no means the only mine in Wales to fuel the Bronze Age.

Beyond the Great Orme

Although the Great Orme is the best preserved of the early copper mines in Wales, it is possible that it was not the greatest. This title may have belonged to Parys Mountain on Anglesey. Between 1768 and 1904, over 3.5 million tonnes of ore were taken from more than 20km of tunnels which honeycomb the mountain, and from the enormous opencast which forms the centrepiece of the mining landscape.

The scale of recent industry has buried much of the original ground surface beneath thousands of tonnes of spoil. But some surface working has survived as both Oliver Davies and Simon Timberlake discovered during their investigations in the 1930s and 1980s respectively. More dramatic though have been the discoveries made by David Jenkins and the Parys Mountain Underground Group who have found several areas where eighteenth century tunnels have cut through earlier workings. As at the Great Orme, this evidence consists of piles of cobbles used as hammerstones, and charcoal from fire setting. Radiocarbon dates show that miners had already reached depths of 30m as early as 1900 BC, long before mining is known to have taken place on the Great Orme.

Mining had also started at Alderley Edge in Cheshire by about 1900 BC. Here Simon Timberlake and the Alderley Edge Landscape Project suggest that early miners were drawn to the site by the presence of green mineralization in the sandstone.

Eighteenth and nineteenth century mining on Parys Mountain (Anglesey).

The massive mining operations which took place over this period have doubtless removed or buried much evidence for earlier quarrying.

© National Museum of Wales (Steve Burrow).

Initial exploitation of these thin layers of malachite led to the digging of several unsuccessful prospection pits, then a rich vertical seam of malachite, azurite, and other copper ores was encountered and subsequently mined.

The north Wales and Cheshire mines are testimony to the importance of this area in the copper trade at this time, but they were not the only areas to be exploited. Work by Simon Timberlake and other members of the Early Mines Research Group has demonstrated early activity at a number of other mines in mid-Wales.

At Nantyrarian spoil suggesting a prospecting trial was dated to around 1800 BC; at Twll y mwyn, at least seven thousand cubic metres of rock were moved at a mine which was probably started before 1750 BC, while at Ogof Wyddon, Nantyreira and Llancynfelin spoil was dated to around 1700 BC. But the most intensively studied site in the region is Copa Hill, where Simon Timberlake began excavating in 1986. Here three or four thousand tonnes of rock were dug out of an opencast trench mine over 10m deep. Mining began in earnest around 2000 BC with the fire setting and quarrying of a 20–30m surface vein of chalcopyrite, some of which had oxidised to malachite. The trench that was created became a water trap leading to drainage problems quite early in the mine's history. To combat this a system of launders was installed to carry the water away.

Unlike the mines of the Great Orme which were worked over an extended period, Copa Hill was exploited for a shorter time and left a much smaller mark on the landscape. It is likely that it was a sideline for farmers or pastoralists, who lived nearer to the coast for much of the year. In the spring they gathered cobbles from the beaches and set off for the mines, 22km to the east, where preserved foliage

Copa Hill (Ceredigion) with the early mine workings in the foreground.
© The National Museum of Wales (Steve Burrow).

Stone hammers used as mining tools on Copa Hill (Ceredigion), including a modern example which demonstrates the way that some may have been hafted.
© The National Museum of Wales (Kevin Thomas).

Original artefacts housed in Amgueddfa Cymru – National Museum Wales.

shows they probably worked throughout the summer. The comparatively small scale of their work does not seem to have impacted greatly on the woodland of the area, nor do significant quantities of heavy metal pollutants seem to have found their way into nearby peat bogs.

The alchemist's art

Arduous as the work at these mines must have been, the extraction of the rock was just the first stage in its conversion to metal, with much subsequent effort focusing on separating ore from the worthless rock and improving its concentration before it was smelted. The best evidence of these processes comes from the Great Orme.

Here the ore was broken up against dressing stones and sorted by hand, before a further stage of crushing using mortars and pestles. When powdered it is likely that the ore was washed to remove the limestone dust. Barbara

Ottaway and Emma Wager of Sheffield University have excavated mine spoil at one site where this may have taken place around 1650 BC, and David Jenkins and Simon Timberlake have identified other likely washing sites close to the coast.

The net result was a concentrated copper ore, ready for smelting. Pure copper melts at 1083 °C, although higher temperatures are needed to ensure that the metal flows and pools into droplets which can be collected after the smelt. These temperatures are far more than can be achieved in an ordinary bonfire, so hand bellows or a well-channelled natural draft were probably needed to force air into the fire and raise the temperature to the necessary level, but here a compromise had to be made. If too much oxygen reached the ore then copper oxide was produced rather than pure copper – a useful pigment, but not something that could be used to make tools. Charcoal provides a remedy for this problem; when it burns it gives off carbon monoxide which 'captures' the free oxygen in the fire, preventing the formation of copper oxide. Alternatively, wood embers burning at the base of a pit may have provided the necessary oxygen-free environment. Either way, smelting on the scale found at the Great Orme would have placed considerable pressures on the local woodland requiring great care in its management if areas were not to be deforested.

The Great Orme (Conwy).

Small streams flowing down the flanks of the mountain were ideal for the washing of copper ore. The edges of this one cuts fine dumps of mine waste which probably result from such activities.

© The National Museum of Wales (Steve Burrow).

Described in this way, smelting appears straightforward, but there are many complicating factors. Different types of ore require different forms of processing. The process described above is applicable to copper carbonates like malachite, which is common on the Great Orme and at Alderley Edge but copper sulphides like chalcopyrite, which are found at other sites, must be repeatedly roasted and smelted to drive off their sulphur. If the smelt is to be successful any other impurities present in the ore must also be removed by the addition of a flux. Silica sand or crushed quartz is added to ores which contain iron; haematite or bog iron is added to those which contain silicates. In both cases the impurities bond with the flux during the smelt to make heavy iron silicates which can be separated from the lighter copper by tapping the base of the furnace. Considerable skill is needed to manage the transition from ore to metal.

Rare proof that smelting took place at the Great Orme rather than further afield has been recovered by Dave

Chapman working at Pen-trwyn headland. In 1997 an eroding layer of burnt material was found to contain copper slag from a furnace lining, as well as tiny fragments of copper metal, from a smelt which had taken place around 1600 BC.

The products of alchemy

The copper age, begun around 2400 BC and described in the previous chapter, did not last long. Pure copper is a soft metal; tools produced from it blunt relatively quickly, necessitating repeated sharpening during use. Arsenical copper of the type produced at Ross Island is harder, but the mixing of about one part tin to ten parts copper makes an even harder alloy: bronze. It is not known whether the early smiths recognised that those who worked bronze were in better health than those who were exposed to arsenic poisoning, but they would surely have appreciated the benefits of working this composite material: the addition of tin lowers the melting point of copper and makes the molten metal more fluid. Technically the resulting bronze would have been superior, but the logistics of its production were complicated at first.

Geevor tin mine (Cornwall).

More recent exploitation of southwest Britain's mineral wealth has probably removed much of the evidence for earlier workings which once existed in this area.

© National Museum of Wales (Steve Burrow).

Turning copper ore into axes.

First, copper ore was crushed to a fine grade and any pieces of rock were separated out and discarded. Ore was then smelted in a bowl hearth, using different heating environments for different types of ore (see text for examples). When sufficient metal had been accumulated by smelting, it was then reheated until molten and poured into a mould.

© The National Museum of Wales (Tony Daly).

Tin is rare in Europe, and the only sizeable concentration in Britain is in southwest England where heavy dark pebbles of tin oxide, known as cassiterite, were probably first found by prospectors scouring streams for gold or copper. Those who collected these pebbles controlled a resource which was to remain vital to the British metal industry for over a millennium. Few traces remain of their endeavours. Some of the best evidence includes tin slag found in a ritual enclosure on Caerloggas Downs near St Austell, and dated by its association with a fragment of a dagger to between 1700 and 1500 BC, and some pebbles of cassiterite found in a settlement at Trevisker, dating to a broadly similar time. But the real proof of Cornwall's importance can be seen in the near ubiquitous occurrence of tin in items made after about 2150 BC.

The necessity of obtaining tin added a new dimension to metal production in Britain and Ireland; even those regions, like Wales, which possessed their own copper ore were reliant on a supply of this material to convert their mineral wealth into bronze. To satisfy demand it would, at first, have been necessary to maintain good relations

with people in southwest Britain or their intermediaries; but as the quantity of bronze in circulation increased, it would have been increasingly possible for those who wanted a new bronze tool to simply melt down an old one.

For those smiths with the necessary raw materials to hand, the next step was to make a mould. The earliest surviving moulds for making axes were pecked and ground into a slab of stone, so that molten metal could be poured in and would spread evenly to form a level surface. Once cool, the object could be removed and hammered to harden the edges and produce the detail of the desired shape.

One of the best preserved moulds from this period was discovered in Walleybourne Brook in Shropshire in 1961. This block of carboniferous grit has matrices for five axes and a rod carved into its sides, and had clearly been used since analysis of the stone showed high levels of copper and tin. Another open mould, found near Betws-y-Coed in Conwy, would have been used to make similarly-shaped axes.

These single piece moulds could only produce relatively flat artefacts, but the ability to make more complex, two-piece, moulds can be inferred from the shape of the many early halberds which are cast with raised ribs running down the length of both sides. With time, smiths also began to make axes in two-piece moulds.

While functional requirements probably fixed the form of the axe within certain parameters, some craftsmen also invested effort in embellishing these functional pieces: decoration reminiscent of raindrops was punched on to some early blades, while diagonal fluted lines can sometimes be seen on the sides of flanged axes. Depictions of axes were also placed in unexpected places, suggesting that for some

Left: Stone mould found at Walleybourne Brook (Shropshire).

© Shrewsbury Museums (Shropshire Museum Service).

Original artefact housed in the collections of Shrewsbury Museums. (23cm long).

Right: Sandstone mould found at New Mills (northern Powys).

This mould would have been used to create blades with an asymmetry reminiscent of halberds.

© The National Museum of Wales (Kevin Thomas).

Original artefact housed in the collections of Amgueddfa Cymru – National Museum Wales. (20.6cm long).

the axe was more than just a tool. The carvings of dozens of axes, a dagger and a knife on the sarsen stones at Stonehenge are perhaps the most famous examples, but carvings of axes and daggers were also found at a cairn at Badbury Rings in Dorset, and axes feature on the capstone of a cist at Nether Largie North in Argyll and Bute. As Stuart Needham first pointed out, the axes are in all cases shown without hafts – functionally worthless, but clearly important to the carver. These haftless depictions suggest that the simple ownership of metal axe blades may have said much about the status of the owner.

By the end of the period covered by this book, there are also instances where significant numbers of metal items are found together – over and above the caches of two or three items noted in previous sections. For example, eight axes were buried in hoards both at Menai Bridge in Anglesey and Moelfre Uchaf in Conwy, and a mix of eight daggers, spears, 'punches' and axes were found at Ebnal in Shropshire. The reason such collections were buried probably varied in each case, but Colin Burgess and David Coombs have suggested four explanations likely to cover most instances. Some hoards may have been buried to conceal their contents, some as offerings to the spirits or gods, some may have been lost by chance, while others might have been kept in pits as a matter of course, only

to be forgotten. Whichever motivations apply to the examples given above, their discovery suggests that the accumulation and perhaps protecting of stocks of metalwork was an important theme of this age.

While metal axes proliferated, halberds declined. Although bronze examples are known in Wales, they seem to have been discarded here as elsewhere in favour of the dagger, a far more familiar weapon to modern eyes and one which avoided the functional problems associated with the long-handled halberd. Bronze was also used to make other items – awls, razors and perhaps tweezers – but like daggers, these are more often found in graves than as stray finds, and so their discussion is reserved for a later chapter.

A new role for the stone workers

The adoption of metal did not mean the instant abandonment of other materials and there is evidence for continued innovation in the design of stone tools, most notably the axe. Returning to the Continent, in Denmark, Germany and central Europe there had been a centuries-old tradition of making heavy axes hafted by a hole drilled through their centre – so called 'axe-hammers'. These were often placed in the graves of men. Many of these continental axes are curved along their length and a similar feature has been noted in examples from Llangollen in Denbighshire, Llanfachreth in Gwynedd and Grondre in Pembrokeshire – raising the possibility that these are directly inspired by European designs. But while the continental burial rite had reached Britain around 2400 BC, it is likely that these and other Welsh examples probably did not appear until a few centuries later. And when these

Axe-hammers were produced with varying degrees of care and elaboration. They range in size from large and heavy, to small and light, with smaller examples being called battle-axes. Miniature examples are illustrated later in this book.

Clockwise from top left, examples from: Bryncroes (Gwynedd); Coedana (Anglesey); Llangwyryfon (Ceredigion); Carno (northern Powys); Llanfyrnach (Pembrokeshire)

© The National Museum of Wales (Kevin Thomas).

Original artefacts housed in the collections of Amgueddfa Cymru – National Museum Wales. (First example, 24.2cm long).

implements were finally taken up it is likely that axe-hammers occupied a niche which complemented rather than competed with metal tools.

The first metal flat axes in Wales weighed on average 0.4kg, although heavier examples are known; as the form of the axe was developed, they became slighter, with later flanged axes weighing considerably less. These figures compare well with those of modern carpentry axes. In contrast, axe-hammers typically weigh about 2.5kg, with examples in excess of 4kg also being known in Wales – figures more closely comparable to modern tree-felling axes or sledgehammers. Whatever their function, a blow from one of these axe-hammers could be delivered with far greater force than could be achieved with a bronze axe. Furthermore, it is entirely predictable that such heavy implements should be made of stone and not bronze. Suitably large pieces of stone were comparatively easy to find, while the effort involved in mining sufficient ore to make a single bronze axe-head would have been very significant. If heavy blades were needed, their production would naturally fall to stone workers and not smiths.

Practical experience has shown that axe-hammers could be used to fell trees, despite their comparatively blunt blades, and experimental archaeologist Dave Weddle highlights one significant benefit that this design of stone axe would have had over the earlier styles. By mounting the head through a central perforation, it could be driven far into the wood without the haft becoming an obstruction, in consequence they were well-designed as splitting axes. The same feature would also have suited them for use as plough blades, and Hubert Savory has suggested that this may have been the function of the worn examples from Anglesey and Llanycil in Gwynedd.

Axe-hammers have also been found in copper-rich areas, and a broken example found at Alderley Edge raises the possibility that they were linked to mining in some way. There is no practical argument against their effectiveness in this role, or in any of the other roles already described. Indeed, the larger examples were probably only suitable for tasks such as these where the blade could be fixed in position, as in the ploughing hypothesis, or used in a simple chopping motion, as in tree felling – they were simply too heavy to be wielded in a more sophisticated manner for any length of time.

Not all are so heavy, and some are works of great craftsmanship, carefully shaped, with bevels on top and bottom, exaggerated shapes to the blade, and with detail carved on their surface. All of this would soon have been obliterated if the tool was swung against a solid target, or ground though the earth. Their fragility in the face of such rough treatment is demonstrated by the fate of an axe-hammer found by a boy at Caer Caradoc in Shropshire. H Noel Jerman wrote in 1934 that the boy

'inserted a stick to act as a handle and proceeded to hit other stones with it until it was broken'.

These smaller examples would have allowed for more versatile usage, and greater control in the swing, with one popular hypothesis leading to their description as weapons – battle-axes – a view which finds support on stelae in northern Italy which are thought to show the axe secured across the chest, and in their presence in the graves of men in northern Europe. There can be no doubt of their effectiveness in this capacity: a single well-placed blow would pulp flesh and shatter bone, without greatly endangering the carefully crafted blade.

The stones from which these axe-hammers and battle-axes were made differed from those used to make the earlier types of stone axes. Early axes were generally made from fine-grained rocks which could be easily flaked, but which would have been very difficult to drill into to make the perforation necessary for these later types. So while a few perforated implements made from Graig Lwyd rock are known, other coarser rocks were now preferred, and two in particular are worth discussing in detail: picrite and spotted dolerite.

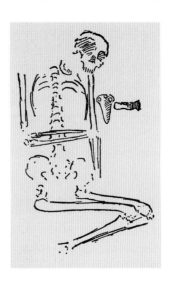

In 1950, Fred Shotton, Lilly Chitty and Wilfred A Seaby announced their discovery that a large number of axe-hammers found in Shropshire and adjacent areas were made from picrite, a comparatively rare rock-type formed during the crystallisation of magma. They identified the source as a low hill near Hyssington in northern

Powys, known erroneously to archaeologists as Cwm Mawr. As well as being suitably coarse and heavy, picrite is a striking and beautiful blue-grey rock which, when polished, is complemented by translucent patches caused by alteration of the mineral olivine.

Although most axe-hammers and battle-axes made from this rock were used close to the production site, some were carried further afield, reaching as far as Cornwall and Lincolnshire. Closer to home, but no less intriguing, Jana Horak has identified one product from Hyssington which was discarded at another picrite source on Anglesey – the two types of picrite may have looked the same to the owner of this implement who perhaps deposited it here in recognition of this similarity. Hyssington axes have also been found in burials in England.

The other noteworthy rock used in the production of axe-hammers and battle-axes, spotted dolerite, is one of the types which were hauled to Stonehenge several hundred years before. Axes made from this material have been found in small numbers across Wales and southern England. Analysis by Olwen Williams-Thorpe and others have shown that while spotted dolerite axe-hammers found in England are of the same rock-types as some of those used at Stonehenge – suggesting a source in the Preseli Hills, or the reuse of the Stonehenge bluestones themselves – those found in Wales are not from the same Preseli sources. Either these examples were derived from nearby, and unidentified sources, or they were made from a similar rock said to exist near Cadair Idris in Gwynedd.

The trade in exotics

Wales was well placed to enjoy the benefits of bronze tools and axe-hammers. The region had abundant copper ore and no shortage of suitable rocks; but it did not have dependable supplies of all the raw materials which were valued at this time. Wales's reliance on tin from Cornwall has already been noted; it was also dependent on other regions for some of the other things valued at this time, notably jet, amber and high quality flint.

Despite the growing importance of bronze during this period, flint continued to be used for the production of small knives, scrapers and arrowheads. In Wales, much of this demand was probably serviced from local beach pebble sources, as it always had been, but a number of flint daggers seem too large to have been made from such source material. In particular, Stephen Aldhouse-Green has suggested that daggers from Ffair Rhos in Ceredigion and Staylittle in northern Powys, were made from flint mined in southern England, while a chert dagger from Candleston in Bridgend hints that these imports were valued enough for some to imitate them in local materials.

It is possible that the use of flint daggers in the centuries around 2100 BC was a consequence of flint knappers imitating the bronze daggers which were becoming more widely available at this time; this seems unlikely, since flint daggers are markedly different in shape from most examples made in bronze. More probably both flint knappers and bronze smiths were attempting to meet a general demand for a close-quarter weapon, and it is only with the benefit of hindsight that one can look back and see flint daggers as the last flash of brilliance from craftsmen working with a declining medium.

The earliest use of jet in Wales dates back to the Gop Cave belt-slider of around 3000 BC, but there was an apparent hiatus in its use for much of the next millennium. This may have been due to a changing political landscape which made it more difficult for people in the west to obtain goods from the Yorkshire coast, or it may have been because people ceased to value it. But jet is found once more in Wales in small quantities after about 2200 BC. Amber, another product from the shores of eastern England, and perhaps sometimes across the North Sea, also appears in small quantities in Wales a little after this. Neither jet nor amber have much practical value (they are essentially ornamental) but they do share the curious electrostatic ability to make hair stand on end, and this may have encouraged demand for beads, buttons and rings made from them.

Like the spread of jet and amber, the continuing spread of gold outside the natural distribution of this material testifies to the value which was placed on ornamental materials at this time. Artefacts made of gold have been found accompanying burials in southern England, most notably in and around Wiltshire. The origin of this obviously imported gold is not known for certain, but since many more gold artefacts have been found in Ireland than in any other potential source region it seems probable that much of it came from there. Even so, the presence of gold in some Welsh streams make it possible that this country also contributed to these patterns of exchange, although proof is elusive.

This swirling trade in materials is a motif of the age: copper and gold moving from west to east, tin from south to north, and amber, jet and fine flint from east to west, yet none of this movement was essential to life. The addition of Cornish tin to Welsh copper produced better tools, but people in Wales could have managed perfectly well without it. What is more, pebble flint from Wales's own beaches could produce edges just as sharp as those provided by daggers made from high quality flint in southern England. When viewed across the broad sweep of history, of equal significance to the materials themselves and the items made from them were the networks by which these materials were acquired. People who coveted their neighbours' possessions were more likely to attempt to satisfy their acquisitiveness. These interactions would, in turn, have encouraged the development of common cultural traditions between regions; one of the products of these interwoven networks was probably the other great motif of the age: a unified approach to the treatment of the dead across the length and breadth of Britain.

The dead in their thousands

It is possible that some limited tool manufacture continued around Graig Lwyd in the centuries after 2200 BC since occasional pieces are found in the soil below later monuments, but the ancient quarries and screes had probably lost much of their significance by this time, becoming lichen-covered and overgrown by grass and scrub. For the most part a mountain which had been quarried for at least a millennia was now just a mountain.

By 1500 BC, however, those who took the trouble to climb its peak would have found it a good vantage point from which to observe another transformation in the use of the surrounding land. To the northeast, the smoke from fire setting would have marked out the mines on the Great Orme, now well-established as an opencast, and with tunnels beginning to penetrate deeper into the heart of the hill. To the south the landscape had been transformed quite differently. About 400m away, on the northern slopes of Moelfre and Cefn Coch, had been built more than a dozen round mounds and a few stone circles. If one climbed Moelfre, many more mounds of earth and stone would have been visible on its far slopes; a short walk further to the south around the flanks of Foel Lwyd and Tal y Fan would have revealed yet more mounds, stone circles and standing stones. The landscape around Graig Lwyd had found a new role and it was not the only landscape in Wales to be treated in this way.

Several of the mounds around Graig Lwyd have been excavated and scores more have been dug across Wales as a whole. The evidence that has been revealed varies from site to site, but an abiding theme unites discoveries at the vast majority: these were burial places, built between about 2200 and 1600 BC, predominately to house cremated remains. Human remains from this period have also been found at stone circles, and associated with standing stones, but at these other sites the remains seem to have bolstered the significance of monuments designed for other purposes. At mounds, death is central and pervasive; after a millennium of concealing the dead, now they were spread across the landscape in conspicuous numbers.

A Wales-wide survey of these monuments commissioned by Cadw has shown that over 4,000 burial mounds – also known as barrows if made from earth or turf, or

© The National Museum of
Wales (Jackie Chadwick,
Tony Daly).

cairns if raised in stone – were built during this period, as well as almost 300 stone, earth and timber circles, and about 1,000 standing stones. They are found in similar numbers in all regions, albeit with variations in the proportions of each type, and occasional localised decreases. In fact, with only a handful of exceptions everyone in Wales lives within a few kilometres of a monument which is proven or suspected

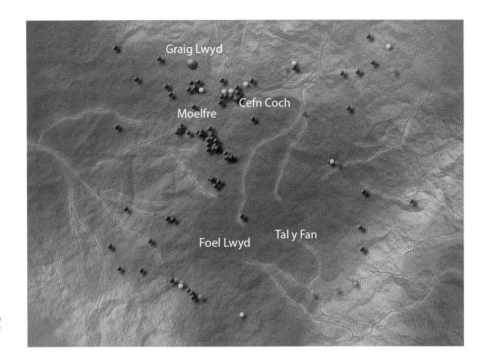

to have been built during this period. Indeed, the only other types of sites to have been built in similar numbers during any other time in Wales's history are chapels and war memorials. And what survives may be just be a fraction of the total number of monuments that were built. Dyfed Archaeological Trust have discovered evidence that hundreds of other sites may have been built in Pembrokeshire alone, their presence now hinted at through place names including elements such as Carn and Carreg (cairn and stone respectively) and in the records of early antiquarians.

Choosing a resting place

Given the sheer number of these monuments, it is likely that many reasons will have influenced their siting. It is noticeable that many were built on land which had been occupied before. In some cases this may have been simply a matter of chance resulting from mound builders choosing areas that had already been cleared of trees, but this is unlikely to have been the case in every instance. At Four Crosses and Trelystan in northern Powys burial mounds were raised over the pit graves of 3000 BC, the small cairn above the latter perhaps providing a visible beacon to which

Distribution of cairns and round barrows in Wales.

Based on site data collected by and © Clwyd-Powys Archaeological Trust, Dyfed Archaeological Trust, Glamorgan-Gwent Archaeological Trust and Gwynedd Archaeological Trust; and map data produced by the Ordnance Survey (reproduced with the permission of Ordnance Survey on behalf of The Controller of Her Majesty's Stationery Office, © Crown copyright 2010).

these later builders returned. At Cefn Caer Euni 1 in Gwynedd, a circle of stones was built over a cluster of stakeholes, a possible hearth, and sherds of Beaker pottery – evidence that this new burial site had been built over an occupation area which had been used after 2400 BC and which may have still been visible on the ground. By building above these earlier sites the mound builders may have been seeking to demonstrate that their own communities had an ancestry in the area.

Other barrows were built with different considerations in mind. Edith Evans of Glamorgan-Gwent Archaeological Trust has shown that a significant number in the uplands of the Glamorgan valleys were positioned on south-facing hill slopes where they would have caught the most sun. The decision seems to have been deliberate, since the majority of hill slopes in the valleys face east or west. It is as though the future needs of the dead for warmth and comfort were being considered. These and many other factors and traditions will have influenced the placing of barrows in other parts of Wales, as the accompanying images demonstrate – by 2000 BC Wales was, after all, a vibrant and complex place.

Comprehensive excavations in the Brenig Valley in Denbighshire by a team coordinated by Frances Lynch offer insights into how just one of these complex burial landscapes came to be filled. Here on the hills overlooking the River Fechan were built at least eleven burial mounds of varying design. Flooding of the valley to make a reservoir prevents appreciation of these monuments as their builders would have seen them, but there can be no doubt that anyone who lived in this area, or who used it as a routeway across Mynydd Hiraethog, would have been well aware of their presence.

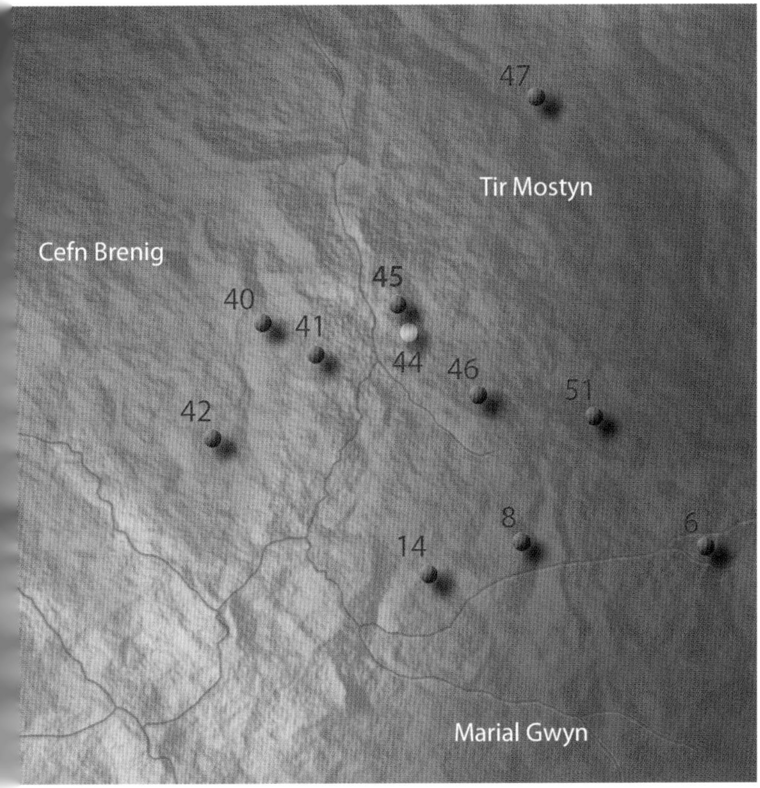

It is difficult to be certain of the order in which these barrows and cairns were erected, but it is likely that two, Brenig 40 and 42, were built at a similar time around 1950 BC. The position upon which Brenig 42 was to sit commanded good views across the valley, and on this spot a circle of stakes 14m in diameter was planted as though to delineate the space for future use. This circle was subsequently taken down and a hurdle-bound fence erected in its place. Within this was set a rectangular wooden structure and, once the deceased had been laid within this, the fence circle was then filled with turves. The whole was then capped with clay to create a mound 19m in diameter. A similar sequence

Distribution of barrows and other monuments in the Brenig Valley (Denbighshire). 40, 41, 42, 45 large barrows; 8, 14, 46 small cairns; 6 small cairn with pronounced kerb; 51 cairn with level platform on top; 44 ring cairn; 47 mound without burials.

Based on site data collected by and © Clwyd-Powys Archaeological Trust, and map data produced by the Ordnance Survey (reproduced with the permission of Ordnance Survey on behalf of The Controller of Her Majesty's Stationery Office, © Crown copyright 2010).

Opposite page from top:

Cairn at Drosgl (Gwynedd).
This cairn was built on the edge of a flat-topped hill. Had it been built at the centre of this 'peak', where this photograph was taken from, the curve of the hill would have given no line-of-sight to the adjacent lowlands. Instead, its off-centre position means it is clearly visible on the skyline when viewed from the adjacent valley. Many barrows and cairns in Wales are built in similar 'false crest' positions, suggesting that they were meant to be visible from specific points in the lowlands – perhaps the location of the mound builders' settlements? The cairn which can be seen today is a reconstruction made after excavation of the site by Peter Crew.
© The National Museum of Wales (Steve Burrow).

Barrow breaking the skyline on the top of Garth Mountain (north Cardiff).
Many burial mounds are built in locations which command wide views – for example, from some on the peaks of the Brecon Beacons one can see mountains as far as 100km away. This example offers views across the whole of Cardiff, and to the Severn Estuary and beyond. It has been argued that such locations were chosen to give the dead a good view of the land, but such considerations only apply on clear days. Often, the hundreds of barrows built on high hilltops would have been enshrouded in clouds, mixing the dead with the sky itself.
© The National Museum of Wales (Steve Burrow).

Barrow at Aber Sychbant (Denbighshire).
Not all burial mounds were built in dramatic locations. This example was situated away from adjacent high ground in a sheltered position on the natural route across the mountains which separate Eglwyseg in Denbighshire from Brymbo in Wrexham.
© The National Museum of Wales (Steve Burrow).

Two Tumps barrows (northern Powys).
This pair of barrows sits at the Welsh end of the Kerry Ridgeway. It is possible that they were intended to mark the start of this route. Several other groups of barrows are known in Wales indicating that some mound builders wanted to place their own dead with deliberate reference to those inhabiting earlier monuments.
© The National Museum of Wales (Steve Burrow).`

Below left: Barrow at Simondston (Glamorgan), under excavation in 1937.
There were few hard and fast rules in barrow building. In many cases, barrows were built in positions which could be easily overlooked – a reversal of the concerns evident in previous examples.
© The National Museum of Wales.

Below right: Ring ditches at St Donats (Glamorgan).
Many barrows were built in the lowlands, in areas which are now subject to arable farming; these face particular threats. This aerial photograph shows two crop circles which mark the location of barrow ditches. The barrows themselves have been destroyed by ploughing.
© Crown copyright (Royal Commission on the Ancient and Historical Monuments of Wales).

 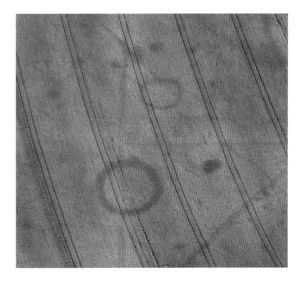

can be seen at Brenig 40 which was built 400m away, also on the western side of the valley. Stake circles also mark the start of the ritual sequence at Brenig 41, a third burial mound nearby.

In all three cases, the mounds seem to have been erected as monuments for individuals, in the case of Brenig 40 an elderly man. But this consistency of one body per mound was not maintained throughout the valley. Parts of one person were found at the centre of another large barrow on the eastern side of the valley, Brenig 45, but the remains of at least six more people were then buried in its flanks; several more were interred in a low platform cairn on the east side of the valley, Brenig 51. As will be seen later in this chapter, these and other burials of this time were treated to a very different funerary rite from the one followed by Beaker users, cremation.

Family mausolea and fields of graves

The repeated use of a single barrow was more common in Wales than the raising of a large burial mound for a single person. While careful excavation has revealed the sequence of burials at many sites, good dating evidence with which to determine the span of time over which a site was used is rarely forthcoming. Two exceptions to this are the burial mounds of Treiorwerth and nearby Bedd Branwen, both on Anglesey, which have been well dated thanks to work by Anna Brindley and Frances Lynch. A dozen or so people were buried at Treiorwerth over perhaps three centuries from

Cists at Capel Cynon (Ceredigion).

Similarities in the design of these two cists, suggest that the same people were involved in their construction.

© The Cambrian Archaeological Association.

about 1900 BC, while about the same number were interred at Bedd Branwen over about 100 years. The similarity of the grave goods found with different burials at these sites suggests that they were used by a single community over these time spans.

The suggestion that these burial mounds were family mausolea has been current among Welsh archaeologists since at least the middle of the nineteenth century and pioneering attempts have been made to explore this hypothesis by studying the DNA of those buried at Bedd Branwen, although insufficient survived to allow conclusions to be

drawn. Looking forward to a time when such analyses are more developed, one deposit where a family relationship between the dead seems very likely is at Tandderwen in Denbighshire. Here an oak coffin carved from a tree trunk was set in a grave. Within the coffin were the cremated remains of two children and a man, and on top of them were placed the remains of a woman, and then another man. The intimacy of the sequence suggests a family returning to a marked burial place.

Some support for the concept of the family mausoleum can be found in the evident care with which old burial mounds were developed over time, with core mounds of turf, soil, or stones, being sealed by layers of clearly different materials, resulting in ever larger monuments. However, not all burial sites from this period fit this model.

Indeed, the remains of many people were probably interred in open cemeteries with no obvious mound above them. Such sites are hard for archaeologists to locate and are easily damaged by ploughing or land development. One example which may have suffered in this regard is Capel Eithin on Anglesey, which was in use for a thousand years from about 2200 BC. Given this extended span of time, one might have expected a large number of burials to have been uncovered when the site was dug in the early 1980s, yet only sixteen separate burials were found, about one for each 60 years of the cemetery's life. It seems surprising that such an infrequently used and unmarked site would have been remembered and returned to over such a long duration – more likely, it was used more often, but subsequent farming of the area has removed all but the most deeply buried remains. Capel Eithin is not alone on Anglesey: just 5.5km to the southwest at Cae Mickney, thirty-two burials were found in 1882 when labourers dug a ditch, and a further seven were discovered a similar distance away at Plas Penrhyn during the building of a tennis court in 1928. The presence of three such cemeteries in an area of just $35km^2$ raises the obvious question as to how many more were once present over the remaining $20,000km^2$ of Wales.

Changing burial rites

This proliferation of burials in mounds and cemeteries was not the only significant change in attitude to death at this time. Equally important was a general shift across Wales which resulted in cremation being adopted as the dominant burial rite at most of the sites described above. Not every community accepted the change however, and some continued to bury their dead as their pre-2200 BC forebears had done. For example, around 2000 BC, at Tandderwen in Denbighshire, a large pit was dug and a coffin placed inside, containing the deceased a Beaker and a flint knife; another grave was dug 5m away and used for similar burial rites. And some time later, at Welsh St Donats 3 in Glamorgan, a woman was buried with a Beaker, a bronze awl, a flint flake and an ox tooth. Although these and

other Beaker burials were superficially the same as those prior to 2200 BC, the increase in quantity and variety of grave goods, suggests that even this now long-established burial rite was undergoing change. Some of these later Beaker users also chose to follow the fashion of the time and build burial mounds to monumentalise their dead, for example at Sutton 268' in Glamorgan, South Hill, Talbenny in Pembrokeshire, Plas Heaton in Denbighshire and Riley's tumulus in Bridgend. In some cases these mounds were subsequently enlarged by communities who had adopted cremation as their burial rite of choice.

Beaker burial found at Sutton 268' (Glamorgan). The white markers indicate the position of the arrowheads found around the skeleton. The excavator, Cyril Fox, believed that the arrows were hafted when they were buried, although the positions of the arrowheads suggest that the hafts may have been snapped.

© The National Museum of Wales.

As time passed the Beaker itself, once a symbol of modernity, became an anachronism in a world where other styles of pottery were now exemplars of the new. Slow creeping change saw more and more of the dead accompanied by jars and vases, with the shape and wide mouths of some of these new pots suggesting that food rather than drink had become important in the burial rite, hence the name given to them by archaeologists, 'Food Vessels'.

The decision to bury the dead with a Food Vessel rather than a Beaker is unlikely to have been a stark or traumatic one for the community. Indeed, other communities

were comfortable burying their dead as corpses without any pot at all, for example at Orseddwen in Wrexham, Corston Beacon in Pembrokeshire, and Cowbridge in Glamorgan, where the dead were apparently just accompanied by daggers. Such variations are perhaps to be expected in a burial tradition which lasted over 600 years. But for many communities these must have seemed just differences of detail, when compared with the decision which others took to switch from inhumation to cremation.

One community which, it could be argued, faced this transition directly, lived near Disgwylfa Fawr in Ceredigion. Here a 2.5m long oak coffin was carved from a tree trunk and set on the ground. No burial survived in this coffin when it was excavated in 1937 – any remains would have long since rotted away – but its length suggests that it was intended to hold an inhumation. A large burial mound, 20m in diameter and over 1.8m high was raised above it. Sometime after the mound was raised, a hole was dug near its top and another oak coffin, just 1m long, was placed in it. Within this was set a Food Vessel, a flint blade and cremated remains. When these burials were interred is not clear – radiocarbon

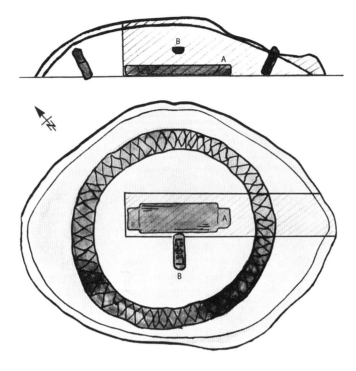

dates from the site do not seem consistent with the archaeological evidence – but the repeated use of oak coffins hints that the burials took place within a relatively short span of time, during which the community altered their treatment of the dead considerably.

Cremation

In more recent times, changes in burial rites in Wales have occurred for a wide variety of reasons, including changes in religious beliefs, issues of public health, increased cultural diversity and the secularisation of death. The reason for the move towards cremation after about 2000 BC is unknown.

It is likely that cremation was viewed as a purifying ritual, releasing the dead from the process of decay and encouraging them towards a spiritual freedom, but it is unlikely that everyone held the same views.

"Did you see the man who was burnt to death?"
"I did not see him. His ghost was not there, his smoke went up to the heavens."

From *The Epic of Gilgamesh*, written about 2050 BC and based on characters who probably lived around 2800 BC.

As the anthropologist Terje Oestigaard has observed, even in our own society many varied perceptions about death are reconciled without difficulty. Some believe the soul goes to heaven, others that it waits on the day of judgment, or that it becomes a ghost, others still that a person simply rots in the ground or burns in the crematorium. If modern society with all the benefits of mass communication can achieve no single view about death and the purpose of burial rites it seems unlikely that people in the past would have done so. However if the reason that cremation was preferred is unknowable, something of the process involved can be recovered. Today cremation is managed with gas and air jets, set within a closed furnace. The temperature and duration of the burn are closely controlled to reflect the size of the individual. When complete, the bones are collected from the furnace before being crushed to a uniform size and released to the relatives of the deceased. In the past, the process would have been much less easy to control, partly due to the available technology, and partly perhaps because of a lack of expertise.

In Nepal, cremations conducted by experienced Hindu priests take between two and three hours, but there is no evidence of a similarly dedicated group of people managing the early cremations in Wales. As a result it may have taken longer for communities to organise themselves on the infrequent occasions when there was a death among their number, and it is more likely that the details of the ceremony would have varied from generation to generation.

The main fuel for the pyre was wood, with Nepalese parallels suggesting that about 300kg would have been needed to cremate an adult, but coal has also been found with cremated remains at Simondston in Glamorgan and Hillbury Barrow in Wrexham. Attendants would have been needed to monitor the fire as it burnt, ensuring that the body was kept in contact with the shifting flames, and that the pyre did not collapse. The difficulties that were faced have been illustrated by Jacqueline McKinley's study of cremated bone from the cemetery at Capel Eithin on Anglesey. Here, blackened tissue, possibly the remains of ligaments, still adhered to some bone which had not been fully cremated, and the bones of the lower spine were consistently under-burnt, since this area was insulated by the soft tissue of the abdomen.

Ceramic cups often featured in cremation rites, ending their days on top of, or mixed among, the cremated remains. The precise purpose of these small vessels is not entirely clear – a fact hinted at by the lack of agreement among archaeologists as to what they should be called: 'pygmy cups', 'accessory vessels' and 'incense cups' have all been proposed for various examples. The last name, suggested by Richard Colt Hoare in the nineteenth century and now rarely used, indicates a belief that

Cup from Sutton 268' (Glamorgan).

This cup was found upside down in the middle of the cremated remains of an eighteen year old individual, probably a man. Fragments from a bone bead and the remains of a bronze knife were also associated with the remains.

© The National Museum of Wales.

Original artefact housed in the collections of Amgueddfa Cymru – National Museum Wales.

Cup from Breach Farm (Glamorgan), with a reconstruction of its original appearance.

Great care went into the making of this cup. It was carefully decorated, and traces of red and white colourants still remain within its incised lines. Work by Mary Davis has shown that these were derived from red ochre and crushed bone.

© The National Museum of Wales (Jackie Chadwick, Kevin Thomas).

Original artefacts housed in the collections of Amgueddfa Cymru – National Museum Wales. (5.1cm tall).

Small pots from sites in Wales.

Many of these cups have two perforations along their middle, as in the examples on the left and centre; some have more extensive latticework holes, as seen on the right.

From left to right: example probably from Ceredigion; Marlborough Grange (Glamorgan); South Hill, Talbenny (Pembrokeshire); Llanarth (Ceredigion); Llanbeblig (Gwynedd).

© The National Museum of Wales (Kevin Thomas).

Original artefacts housed in the collections of Amgueddfa Cymru – National Museum Wales. (Largest example, 6.5cm tall).

these pots were used to waft incense at the pyre side, an opinion which draws on the frequent presence of multiple perforations in the sides of these vessels, as though they were intended to be hung like church incense burners. Other cups are cut by lattice work as if to encourage air flow to the burning contents. Certainly, it would seem appropriate for incense to have formed a part of burial rituals which themselves saw the conversion of the flesh of the dead into smoke, but chemical analysis of cups from across Britain by Alex Gibson and Ben Stern has not found any surviving residue to support this theory. William Owen Stanley, the nineteenth century antiquarian, took the debate in a different direction with a suggestion that the vessels may have been used to hold the flame with which the pyre was lit. The discovery of dry charcoal beneath a cup found at Bedd Branwen on Anglesey could be seen as supporting his theory, although final proof is likely to evade this theory, as it has done all others, to date.

The dead were probably cremated clothed, or perhaps covered by shrouds, and with possessions familiar to them in life. Burnt points made from bone have been found mixed with cremated remains; these may have held hair or coverings in place before the flames took hold. Other possessions which accompanied the dead onto the funeral pyre included dagger pommels, belt hooks and beads. In consigning these items, as well as the clothes themselves, to the flames, communities were giving up prized objects in their efforts to honour the dead. The cremation ceremony may also have been a time of feasting, with burnt pig and cattle bones sometimes being mingled with the remains.

The burning of the pyre was itself a very public display. Smoke would have been visible for many miles on a windless day, and the flames would have burned brightly at night. When it was over, a successful cremation would have reduced the body to brittle fragments of mineralised bone mixed in a mass of ash, charcoal and part-burnt wood which in some cases was gathered up and buried without further ceremony. In other cases, as at Drosgl B in Gwynedd, the bones were buried clean. The fastest way to achieve this end would have been to shovel up both ash and bone and drop it into a pot of water to separate the two; the laborious alternative was to collect the bones by hand.

In all cases, the difficulties involved in gathering every last fragment of bone from the mess of the pyre would have been considerable. While Jacqueline McKinley notes that cremation reduces the average-sized adult to a pile of about 3kg of bone, a review of cremation deposits found in Wales by Frances Lynch suggests that few were recovered from the pyre in their entirety; indeed sometimes only a token amount was kept.

Laying the dead to rest

The comfort and grandeur of the deceased's final resting place varied. Wooden structures built to house the dead are well-known in Wales. In addition to the oak coffins at Disgwylfa Fawr, a burial accompanied by a Beaker was placed in a lidded wooden coffin at Tandderwen, its location possibly marked by a post. The grave shaft was subsequently dug into by later grave diggers who placed their own hollowed-out log into the pit they had made. These, and other suggestions of wooden coffins, are doubtless just the lucky survivors of a tradition of coffin-use which must once have been common, but inevitably the durability of rock means that it is the stone cists which survive in greater numbers.

The use of cists, first noted around 2400 BC, continued until the end of the period covered by this book, but their role changed with developments in burial rites. The basic limitations imposed by the size of the body meant that cists which were to house inhumations could not be much smaller than about 0.9 by 0.6 by 0.6m. Indeed, when bodies were laid stretched out on their backs, as in a burial at Corston Beacon in Pembrokeshire, an even longer cist was needed.

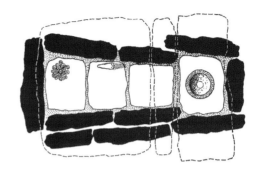

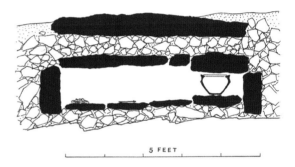

Once a community had switched to cremation there was no longer a functional requirement for a cist to be body-sized, yet many large cists have been found which only contain cremated bone, such as the 1.5m long cist at Candleston Castle in Bridgend which held a cremation, bronze dagger and Food Vessel. It is possible that this is an instance where an old cist made to hold an inhumation had been reused, the former occupant either being removed, or having since decomposed completely. Evidence to support this theory was found at Carneddau 1 in northern Powys, where high phosphate levels within a modest-sized cist suggest that a fully fleshed body had once been interred there, although all that excavation found were the cremated remains of a woman. This need not have been the case in every instance, and it is possible that some large cists like the one at Candleston were built to give the cremated dead as much space as they would have needed in life, regardless of their current reduced state. Alternatively, the large cist may have been needed to house organic offerings which accompanied the cremated remains, and of which no trace survives.

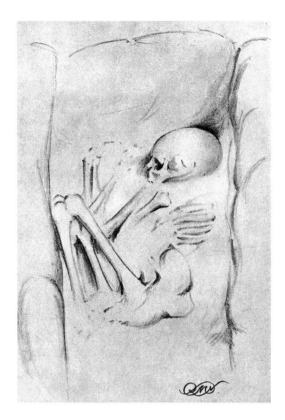

In general though, the opportunity which cremation offered to reduce the size of the cist seems to have been taken – doubtless smaller pieces of stone were easier to come by than large ones – and in some cases the cist was reduced in size and quality until it became little more than shoring to hold back the soil around the remains. One twist in the diminution of cist size can be seen at Ystrad-Hynod in northern Powys, where a 30cm square cist was built to house the cremated remains of a woman, but her bones were imperfectly burnt and some had been broken as though they were forced into the confined space.

Urn burial

In a growing number of cases after 2200 BC, the cist was supplemented or replaced by another way of protecting the remains of the dead: the burial urn. While Beakers and Food Vessels seem to have been developed by communities whose burial rites were rooted in a tradition of inhumation, the burial urn seems better designed for the requirements of cremation.

Burial found at Pwll Swill (Bridgend).

The tightly-bundled body shown in this sketch may have been deliberately bound – another method of fitting a large corpse into a small space.

In the traditions of the Indian Rig Veda, which date to before 1000 BC, burial urns are described as houses of clay, an analogy which seems appropriate here, especially when one considers the scale of larger examples like the 52cm tall Collared Urn found at Carneddau 1 in northern Powys. Given their size and relative fragility it seems likely that most were made close to the place at which they were buried – the product perhaps of the communities whose dead were interred inside them – but this was not always the case. Analysis by David Jenkins and John Ll Williams of stone fragments in urns from Cae Mickney and Llanddyfnan (both on Anglesey), found they contained hypersthene microdiorite, a rock found 20 to 30km away across the Menai Straits at Penmaenmawr. In an even more extreme case, urns found at Brenig in Denbighshire were made from materials which may have been collected as far afield as the Malvern Hills, over 120km away. In these and other instances one is left to wonder whether the communities which used these urns were importing crushed stone from far afield and making the pots themselves, or whether the finished pots were carried, carefully, over great distances; and if so, why?

Top left: Urn from Sheeplays Farm (Glamorgan).

Several different styles of urn accompanied burials at this time. Most common in Britain are so-called 'Collared Urns' like this one, of which a survey published in 1984 recorded almost 2,200 examples.

The thick collared rims and the upper parts of these vessels are often decorated with marks made by pressing cord into clay, or by cutting the pot's surface, generally with straight lines which are often arranged to make zig-zag patterns.

© The National Museum of Wales (Kevin Thomas).

Original artefact housed in the collections of Amgueddfa Cymru – National Museum Wales. (30.5cm tall).

Top right: Urn from Clocaenog (Denbighshire).

Some urns, like this one, have forms reminiscent of Food Vessels, hence the name given to them, 'Food Vessel Urns'. These are themselves similar to urns made in Ireland, hinting at cultural links between these regions.

© The National Museum of Wales (Kevin Thomas).

Original artefact housed in the collections of Amgueddfa Cymru – National Museum Wales. (32cm tall).

Right: Urn from Penllwyn Methodist Chapel (Ceredigion), found in a cist by a man digging a grave.

The decoration on this vessel, which is known as an 'Encrusted Urn' is very different from that found on Collared Urns, Food Vessels or Beakers. The ornament is formed of spattered lumpish decoration, including zig-zagging or curving ribs of clay, with raised circles between them. Since only a few Encrusted Urns have been found in Wales, it is possible that they were viewed as too different from the norm for them to be widely adopted here.

© The National Museum of Wales (Kevin Thomas).

Original artefact housed in the collections of Amgueddfa Cymru – National Museum Wales. (34.6cm tall).

*Cup from Whitford,
(Flintshire).*

*Not all the vessels which
accompanied the dead were
finely finished pieces. This
small example is little more
than a rough pinch-pot
drawn from a lump of clay,
with little effort to elaborate
on its form. Was this the work
of an inexpert potter, or a
craftsperson in a hurry?*

© The National Museum of
Wales (Kevin Thomas).

Original artefact housed in
the collections of Amgueddfa
Cymru – National Museum
Wales. (6.8cm tall).

*Urns from Capel Eithin
(Anglesey).*

*This group of urns, many of
which have lost their bases
to the plough, illustrates the
variety of shapes and designs
in use in a single burial
ground. Despite the great
number of urns which have
been found, often several
to a site, it is very difficult to
identify more than one as
being the products of a single
potter. Rare exceptions can
be seen at Bedd Branwen
and Cae Mickney, both on
Anglesey, where two pots
seem to have been made by
the same hand.*

© The National Museum of
Wales.

Original artefacts housed in the
collections of Oriel Ynys Môn.
(Diameter of largest urn's mouth,
about 29cm).

Urn from Capel Eithin (Anglesey).

Perfection was not key to the successful interment of the dead, and some communities clearly adopted a make-do-and-mend attitude to the use of burial urns. This Collared Urn had been allowed to slump before it was fired giving it an awkward lop-sided appearance. Other urns were used which had already been chipped around their rim, as at Treiorwerth on Anglesey and Ysgwennant in northern Powys, or which had cracked and required repair, as at Carneddau 1 in northern Powys and Fan y Big in southern Powys. Clearly seconds were considered appropriate at the grave side.

© The National Museum of Wales.

Original artefact housed in the collections of Oriel Ynys Môn. (about 29cm tall).

Llanbadarn Fawr (Ceredigion).

In the 1920s Mortimer Wheeler, then of the National Museum of Wales, reconstructed an urn of uncertain provenance which was in the collections of University College Museum, Aberystwyth. It was only in 1932 that Iorwerth Peate, also of the museum, became aware that the finder of the urn had had its image carved on his tombstone along with an inscription that described its discovery in the parish of Llanfihangel-y-Creuddyn in 1840.

© The National Museum of Wales (Steve Burrow).

While cists and urns were regularly used, they were not felt necessary in all funerals. Many cremated remains are found without any protective covering, just contained within scoops in the ground, or dug into the side of barrows. Some of these simple burials are found in discrete piles, suggesting they were stored in skin bags or baskets which have since rotted away. Storage in a soft bag prior to burial will have offered little protection to fragile cremated bones, which may explain well-crushed remains found at sites like Llanilar in Ceredigion and Trelystan in northern Powys.

Other cremation deposits were not even afforded the protection of a bag, being discovered as dispersed spreads in the ground. Sometimes this is the result of later disturbance, but an example from Tandderwen in Denbighshire demonstrates that this could be intentional. Here, cremated bone was simply tipped into a pit, leaving a trail up one side. One is left to wonder whether the living did not value these dead enough to afford them more honour, or whether honour was ascribed to them in other ways before their remains were interred.

Who was buried

The identity of the dead has been of great interest since the beginnings of archaeological research in Wales. Before a clear grasp of Welsh chronology had been obtained, many scholars sought to link their discoveries with written records, and the store of Welsh literature, stretching back to the 6th century AD, provided them with a rich reserve of names, deeds, and burial places with which to attempt this task.

Perhaps the most famous instance of this erroneous compounding of prehistoric archaeology and medieval literature came in 1813 when a cremation deposit was found under an urn in a cist beside the banks of the Alaw River in Anglesey. Those who saw it were reminded of the tale of Bronwen which forms part of the medieval prose tales, popularised as the Mabinogion: 'A square grave was made for Bronwen, the daughter of Llyr, on the banks of the Alaw, and there she was buried.' It seemed that one of Wales's legendary heroines had been discovered. The 'discovery of Bronwen' was accepted by Welsh antiquarians for many years, before sober reflection and the weight of evidence led to the recognition that these remains, and all the others found in urns predated Welsh literature by millennia. But this desire to link these burials with known history was pervasive and understandable. As Sir Richard Colt Hoare, one of the leading antiquarians of the early nineteenth century, wrote:

> [before the discovery of Bronwen] I had often reason to lament, that, by their contents, we could form no conjecture, either at what period, or to what personage, the sepulchral tumulus was raised.

Fuelled by analogies from both Welsh and classical literature it is inevitable that throughout the nineteenth century burials, especially those found in barrows, should have been interpreted as the remains of the elite, and discussions were peppered with titles like king, chieftain and druid.

Discoveries made at Mold in Flintshire seemed to offer support to this view. Here on 11 October 1833, workmen dug a hole beside the Chester to Mold road, now the A541. A local landowner ordered the hole to be filled in by shovelling stone from a mound beside the road, and during their work the men came upon part of a skeleton and the largest single gold item from this time ever found in Britain, the Mold Cape. This single sheet of beaten gold, impressed with lines suggesting beadwork, was shaped to cover the shoulders and upper torso in a glittering display; upon it were rows of up to three hundred amber beads. Coarse cloth was found on the cape and perforations at the cape's base suggest that more cloth was sewn on either to form a fringe, to line its inside, or perhaps to make a longer garment.

At the time of discovery, scholars looked at this splendour and assumed that here were the remains of a great man, a belief perpetuated until quite recently when the now obvious question was posed: could the wearer not have been a woman?

The discovery of the Mold Cape in 1833.

Upon discovery of the cape, the landowner threw it into a hedge until work was finished for the day, during this time it was picked at by onlookers some of whom subsequently recast the pilfered gold into rings and pins. Just one of the many beads was preserved. The site of the discovery is now marked with a plaque, but the find spot itself does not survive.

The age of the Mold Cape has been a matter for debate. The style of ornament has led some to argue that it was made around 1200 BC, but more recent analysis by Stuart Needham suggests that a date between 1900 and 1600 BC is more likely.

Original artefact housed in the collections of the British Museum.

Whichever was the case, the cape has fascinated archaeologists and the public ever since. Nothing else like it has been discovered making it difficult to be certain of its original form or purpose. The battered and twisted remnants have led some to suggest that it was a corselet, while in the 1920s it was argued that it was the breastplate of a horse. It was only in the 1950s that A H A Hogg and T G E Powell concluded independently that the pieces were more likely to have formed a cape. This cape would have been awkward for its wearer since their arms would have been tightly constrained, limiting the amount of movement in their upper body. With this in mind, and considering also that it was found on a corpse, it is possible that it was never intended to be worn in life, but was part of a very elaborate shroud. But a counter-argument can be made since the cape itself shows sign of repair along its lower edge, suggesting that it may have been in use for some time before burial.

The sheer splendour of the Mold Cape, augmented as it was by hundreds of imported amber beads, argues strongly for the importance of its wearer, although it can be noted that the dead do not dress themselves and the cape may say more about the status of the mourners than it does about the deceased. But the Mold Cape is an exception. Most burials from this time are accompanied by few, if any, possessions making it hard to make comment about their status in life, just as it would be difficult to identify the great and the good from the bones found in a Christian cemetery. Furthermore, with cremation the dominant burial rite, the people of this time have only been offered a crippled immortality. Although the small size of cremated remains and their resistance to decay in acidic soils has aided their preservation in large numbers, the crushed and distorted state has eroded much of the biography that would otherwise be written into the surfaces of their bones or locked within their molecular structures. Nonetheless, with skill it is sometimes possible to learn something about the deceased.

Young and old

Despite early expectations, not everyone who was buried was a leader. Many children are known to have been cremated which is in itself a point of interest. Infant mortality must have been very high at this time, as it was until the beginning of the twentieth century, and some past societies, notably ancient Rome, responded by denying children the burial rites of adults until they had survived their first difficult months. There seems to have been no such reservation in Wales. At Brenig 45 in Denbighshire a child of less than six months was cremated and laid to rest in an urn, and a cremated newborn was buried in a Food Vessel at Tandderwen, 13km to the south. These cremations would have required the same attention to the pyre

as would the cremation of an adult, and the same effort in collecting the remains. The death of a child was clearly felt to require ceremony, and some families even went to the length of setting their children at the heart of new monuments. For example, at Welsh St Donats 2 in Glamorgan, an infant less than a year old was cremated and buried in a pot, their resting place being marked by the building of a small cairn.

It is likely that more children were cremated by grieving families than excavated instances suggest. Children's bones are less likely to survive the cremation fires than those of adults, and many would have been reduced to ash by the flames. Children's ear bones will have been the most resilient part of their skeletons and these are the only remains to have survived of cremation deposits found at Bedd Branwen and Treiorwerth on Anglesey.

Jacqueline McKinley of Wessex Archaeology has noted that within tight-knit communities children would rarely have been out of sight, raising the possibility that some may have felt it appropriate to bury a child with an adult who could continue to 'care' for them. Certainly many instances are known of children being buried with other people, presumably members of their extended family. In some cases this will have been the result of a common tragedy, as at Sutton 268' in Glamorgan where the cremated remains of a woman were found with those of a foetus or newborn suggesting death in childbirth. In other cases, the bones of a child may have been kept until a companion could be found for them in death.

Men and women are also found buried together. At Trelystan 1 in northern Powys, a woman aged about twenty and a man over thirty were interred together. At Ffridd y Garreg Wen in Flintshire and Treiorwerth on Anglesey burials containing both men and women have also been found. The inference that these are the remains of couples is natural, if unproven.

In general the burial rite seems to have treated all equally and, without accompanying grave goods or the specialist eye of an osteoarchaeologist, it is rarely possible to know whether a man or woman is present in any particular case. The burial ground at Capel Eithin on Anglesey provides a possible exception, with evidence hinting that men and women may have been treated differently during their interment. Across Wales, urns are variously buried upright, with the cremated bone set inside, or placed upside down to form a cover over the bone pile. At Capel Eithin the remains of five men and four women have been tentatively identified within eighteen cremation deposits – the remaining bone belonging either to children or being unidentifiable. All five of the men were buried below upturned urns, and three of the four women were buried in upright urns. The neatness of this picture is only marred by the fourth woman who was in an upturned urn.

If one collates existing records – some of dubious reliability – there is a hint that this distinction was observed across Wales, with men having been identified below upturned urns at Afon Wen in Gwynedd, Bedd Branwen on Anglesey, Brenig 45 and Tandderwen in Denbighshire, Carneddau 1 and 2 in northern Powys and at Kilpaison Burrows in Pembrokeshire; and women within upright urns at Llanilar in Ceredigion, Ty'n-y-Pwll on Anglesey and Ysceifiog in Flintshire. Again, the picture is not perfect: an upright urn found at Goodwin's Row Barrow in Carmarthenshire contained the cremated remains of a man, and upturned urns at Kilpaison Burrows and Merddyn Gwyn on Anglesey are both said to have covered the remains of women. But such ambiguity need not disprove the point; the burial tradition described here lasted for centuries and encompassed the funerary rites of hundreds of small communities.

What the dead took with them

....

Throughout previous chapters mention has been made of objects found with the dead in their graves. It is not known for certain why grave goods – a delightfully serious name – were included. They may indicate the role the deceased played in life: a warrior buried with his weapons, a bronze smith with his tools. They may also be indicators of an imagined afterlife in which physical possessions would still be needed; but this need not necessarily be the case. Everything included with the dead was selected by those who survived them. In some cases they may have chosen items for which they had no more use, as token offerings, in others they may have selected things of great value to demonstrate their respect for the deceased. Yet despite these difficulties of interpretation, the grave does provide a sealed time capsule linking items with the communities that produced them and, regardless of their relationship to the dead, they are a valuable resource in the task of fleshing out the bones of society at this time.

The bare necessities

Flint flakes have been found with a range of burials in Wales. At one level these items are commonplace and unremarkable, but in their day they were no less important for that. Their sharp edges offered the easiest way to cut wood, reeds, hides, meat and other organic materials, and it is likely that most people would have had at least one, whether for making new tools, repairing old possessions, or just for cutting up their food. Examples include a flint knife and a flake which had been damaged during use, both found with a woman at Carneddau 1 in northern Powys, and flakes which accompanied individuals on to the funeral pyre, at Capel Eithin on Anglesey and Garthbeibio in northern Powys.

A tool for piercing was probably valued almost as much as a cutting blade – without one it would be impossible to bore holes in a hide to make clothes, bags or larger objects. In previous ages, bone, antler or flint points served these roles, and doubtless they were still used, but metal was also well-suited to such tasks and bronze points, or awls, are common finds from this time. Although bone points may have been

much easier to make or acquire than bronze ones, the slender profile and durability of a bronze point will have conferred functional benefits for some tasks. But not all metal awls were equally robust as the owner of one from Cae Mickney on Anglesey may have discovered; theirs was made from copper and lead which, as Frances Lynch argues, would probably have been too soft to withstand much pressure on its tip. It can be speculated that the owner of the sub-standard Cae Mickney awl was probably a woman since awls are normally found in women's graves, as at Ystrad-Hynod in northern Powys, Riversdale in Cardiff and Welsh St Donats 3 in Glamorgan. Not all awls need necessarily have been women's tools however, as an example found with the remains of a man and child at Capel Eithin suggests.

Longer points and awls – particularly examples made from bone and antler – may also have served as fasteners, with burnt examples from sites like Capel Eithin and Fan Foel in Carmarthenshire probably serving to pin the clothes, or hold closed the shrouds of the dead as they lay on the pyre. One bronze awl found at Simondston in Glamorgan may also have been used to pin closed a bag containing cremated bone, although this is unlikely to have been its original function.

While the versatility of points and awls may have been their chief value, a few examples are of more complex design, suggesting that they served more specific functions. These include perforated bone pins found with cremated remains at

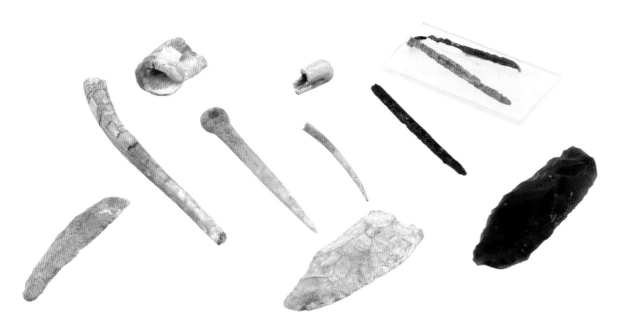

Tredunnock in Monmouthshire, and Golden Mile and Welsh St Donats (both in Glamorgan) which bear comparison with modern needles, although the heads on the last two are too large to pass through fine fabric. Alternatively, it is possible that they were used as clothes pins, with thread looped through the hole and around their tip to secure them in place. A still more elaborate example with a three-lobed head was found at Bryn Crug in Gwynedd, its form suggesting use as a decorative dress pin.

Other types of fasteners are also known from this time. Unique in Wales is a decorated bone belt hook, found in a deposit of cremated bone at Fan Foel in Carmarthenshire; this object would have been fixed to one end of a belt, for hooking onto a loop at the other end. An alternative form of belt fastener is known from a grave at Ysgwennant in northern Powys, consisting of two jet rings. These would originally have been attached to belts by fixing threads through holes in their sides. Small buttons, with a V-perforation at their base, and mostly made of jet, were also used, with one well-worn example from Four Crosses in northern Powys being found in the chest area of a skeleton. Others from Pen y Bonc on Anglesey and Ysgwennant fastened a necklace and pouch respectively, demonstrating once again the varied roles to which the same items might be put.

Button and dagger from a burial at Merddyn Gwyn (Anglesey).

The wear on this button suggests it was used for some time before burial.

© The National Museum Wales (Steve Burrow).

Original artefacts housed in the collections of Bangor Museum. (Button, 3cm diameter).

Clothing and coverings

The materials which these items secured, or onto which they were sewn, remain largely a matter of speculation. Perhaps the best indication of the type of practical workaday clothing which might have been worn by a person walking in the mountains of Wales around 2200 BC, comes from the body of an ill-fated traveller, the 'Ice Man', who died in the Alps a thousand years before. With the exception of the Ice Man's grass cape his clothing was made entirely of animal skins, for the most part goat. The image of a skin-clad traveller may suggest a primitive creature, crude and unsavoury, but these were not skins thrown across the shoulders, but sewn leggings, and a carefully patterned coat. Nor were the raw materials involved of trivial importance; reconstruction of the Ice Man's clothing show that up to eleven goats may have been killed to provide the necessary materials, no small investment and an indication that clothing was probably treated with care and repeatedly repaired to extend its useful life.

Wales has yet to produce a similarly well-preserved set of clothes, although it is possible that such items survive in the anaerobic conditions of its older bogs; instead the direct evidence for skins or fabrics of any kind is restricted to chance survivals in less favourable conditions. For example, animal skin from a grave at Disgwylfa Fawr in Ceredigion which may have once covered the dead; and hair or fur found on the blade of a bronze knife at Welsh St Donats 3 in Glamorgan, possibly the remains of a scabbard or sheath. A flint dagger from Ffair Rhos in Ceredigion also had traces of polish on its edges, which may have been derived from repeated contact with a leather sheath.

Plant fibres were also found on the Ffair Rhos knife, a faint hint of what were probably the most important and easily

Left: The patterns found on ceramics of this period are of a type which could have been easily replicated in other materials such as textiles or basketry, as demonstrated here in this collection of designs used by Indians of the Yakama Nation.

© Barry Friedman.

Right: Some pots like these from Brynford, Flintshire (top), and Clocaenog, Denbighshire (bottom), are decorated with raised strips, suggesting straps or handles. It is possible that they mirror in clay the appearance of basketry from this period.

© The National Museum of Wales (Kevin Thomas).

Original artefacts housed in the collections of Amgueddfa Cymru – National Museum Wales.

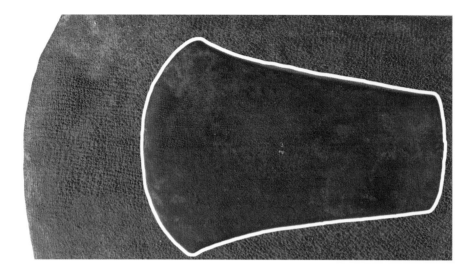

obtainable materials for cordage and textiles. Useful fibres included those from below the bark of small-leaved lime trees, from nettles, or from flax which could be processed to make linen. One of these fibres probably went to make the 'coarse cloth' found with the Mold Cape burial in 1833, and which was noted as being arranged as braiding either across or at the base of the cape. Woven material also accompanied cremated remains excavated at Mynydd Epynt in southern Powys. Neither textile now survives; instead, archaeologists work with the ghosted impressions of fabrics which are preserved in other materials. One such woven impression was found on the rim of an urn excavated at Bryn Bugailen Fawr in Denbighshire in 1851. This was assumed to be evidence for a fabric lid, but since the impression must predate the firing of the pot it is more likely to be derived from a cloth upon which the vessel was placed to dry.

The items of which these textiles may have been a part can be inferred from study of slightly later Danish coffin burials. Conditions inside these wooden coffins were such as to preserve close-fitting blouses, short string-skirts and longer blanket-like woven skirts, as well as hair nets, caps, belts, loincloths and leather shoes. Items were made from both linen and wool, with skin and fur also being used. It seems unlikely that fine clothes would have been worn while hard at work, but this evidence certainly hints at what people in Wales might have considered to be the period equivalent of Sunday best.

Beautifying the body

Clothing, of whatever material, offered a canvas to be decorated and there seems no reason to doubt that the opportunity was often taken, whether by selecting contrasting colours, or by sewing on tassels, feathers, or other ornaments, including the V-perforated buttons already described. Previous chapters have also shown that common tools were also elaborated so that they too became objects of beauty and value. But tools and clothing had their roots in functional requirements, jewellery did not, its very purpose was to make its wearer feel and appear beautiful and exotic.

Body adornment using jewellery seems to have become a serious business after 2400 BC. One-off items are found in Wales prior to this time, but afterwards ornaments began to appear in forms which are recognisable across Britain and Ireland, notably lunulae and bead necklaces.

Gold lunulae are common in Ireland, but only a single specimen has been recorded from Wales, from Llanllyfni in Gwynedd. It is thought that they were worn as collars or rigid necklaces, although in her review of lunulae, Joan Taylor has noted that many appear unworn, suggesting that they were used infrequently, or perhaps that they adorned statues rather than people. Intriguingly, lunulae are not found

Two pottery studs, a flint knife and cup, found with cremated remains at Brenig 44 (Denbighshire).

Similar studs have been found beside the head of burials at other sites, raising the possibility that they were worn in the ear.

© The National Museum of Wales (Steve Burrow).

Replicas displayed at Brenig Visitor Centre. (Largest ear stud, 3cm diameter).

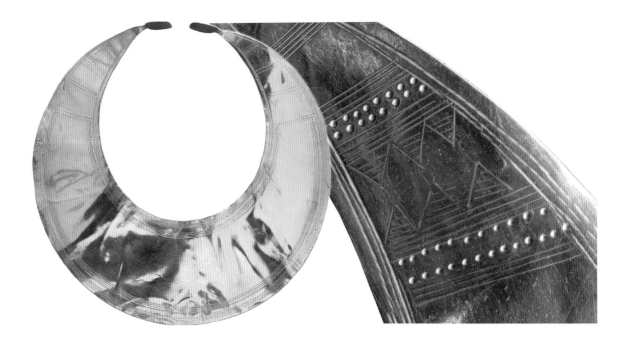

in graves, raising the possibility that their owners deliberately abandoned them in other rituals. It is perhaps significant therefore that the Llanllyfni lunula was found by chance in a peat bog.

The distribution of gold lunulae reflects, in broad terms, the availability of gold in the west of Britain and Ireland. Some time after their initial development, raw materials more readily available in eastern Britain began to be used to similar ends: from Yorkshire came multi-stranded jet necklaces and, later still, in southern England, amber necklaces became popular. Two necklaces of jet, or jet-like materials, have been found in Wales, from Pen y Bonc on Anglesey and Llong in Flintshire; other single and small groups of beads are known. The Mold Cape burial has produced the greatest number of amber beads – reportedly over three hundred, presumably arranged as a necklace – with a few other beads being known from other sites.

While lunulae are largely recovered as stray finds, necklaces are often found with inhumation burials. This was probably the case with the multi-stranded Pen y Bonc necklace which was found in 1828 in a cist, with unconfirmed accounts stating that bronze armlets and a penny were also present, the latter presumably dropped by one of the finders.

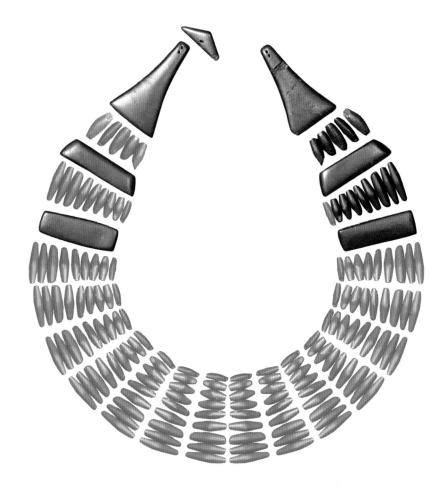

Pieces from a jet necklace found at Pen y Bonc (Anglesey), arranged as part of a speculative reconstruction.

The surviving parts of this necklace consist of plates, perforated to hold strings which served to separate the multiple strands of the necklace, and a button serving as a fastener. Only thirteen beads were present out of the dozens which would have been needed to complete the original design. Whether the missing beads were made of an organic material which had rotted away, or whether this is all that were placed in the grave is not known.

© The National Museum of Wales (Kevin Thomas).

Original artefact in the collections of The British Museum, currently on loan to Amgueddfa Cymru – National Museum Wales.

Work by Mary Davis and Alison Sheridan has shown that most of the surviving parts of this necklace were made of a dark stone, in imitation of jet, but one bead and the button were of the genuine Yorkshire-sourced material. Sheridan goes on to argue that the necklace was probably made in Wales with the jet bead and button being taken from another necklace when the original pieces broke. The other dark-stone necklace from Wales, found in a burial mound at Llong in Flintshire, is rather different. It consists of over 950 small disc-shaped beads, mixed with four larger beads and a spacer plate made of a darker material, possibly jet. As at Pen y Bonc, this mixing and matching of beads of different materials and types may have been a consequence of wear and tear leading to the need to replace damaged items. Such problems were not faced by owners of gold jewellery who could melt down their possessions and start again, assuming they had the skill for the task.

Necklace from Llong (Flintshire).

© The National Museum of Wales (Steve Burrow).

Original artefacts housed in the collections of Flintshire Museum Service. (Largest piece, 3.3cm long).

The Lady of Llong (Flintshire), found buried below a small cairn.

© Flintshire Museum Service.

In the rest of Britain, necklaces are more often found in the graves of women than of men, and this fits the modern perception of who normally wears jewellery, but in Wales the evidence is equivocal on this subject. Nothing survived of the person buried with the Pen y Bonc necklace, while at Llong a woman *was* buried in a grave which was covered by turf and a small cairn, but the necklace was found in this cairn, not with the woman, and subsequent burials on the site add complications to the question of ownership. The gender of the wearer of the Mold Cape, with their 300 amber beads, is also unknown. Indeed, the only instances where bone survives to tell of the sex of the jewellery's owners – at Sutton 268' in Glamorgan where a single bone bead was found, and at Bedd Branwen on Anglesey where ten beads of cannel coal and amber were recovered – they were found to have accompanied men. Clearly jewellery was not just the preserve of women at this time.

It is notable that bronze was not used to make jewellery in Wales, unless one accepts the unverifiable account of a bronze armlet being found at Pen y Bonc, but metals were involved in the production of beads of another material: faience. This is made from an unprepossessing mix of crushed sand or siliceous stone, copper-based colourant and plant ash, bound into a paste with an organic binder and fired until the ingredients fuse to make a grey / blue or turquoise glass-like material. In most cases their original beauty has suffered as a result of surface degradation and the ravages of the funerary pyre through which many of the surviving beads have passed.

Bronze was occasionally used to make items for the control of body or facial hair, notably razors. The discovery of these tools for grooming at sites across Britain and Ireland suggests a general concern with the beautification of the body, invoking images of carefully groomed people, but the context in which much of this equipment is found is the usual dismal one – the grave – raising the possibility that shaving might actually have been part of the funeral ritual, perhaps as part of the purification of the deceased or a cleansing of the mourners. Support for this latter view comes from a burial at Winterslow in Wiltshire where a collection of facial hair was found mixed with cremated bone.

Razors remain rare in Wales and those found are often badly damaged, for instance the decorated example from the top of a burial mound at Welsh St Donats 3 in Glamorgan, and another possible one, damaged and twisted in the heat of a cremation pyre, found at Llanddyfnan on Anglesey. Nonetheless, they are present, and a further suggestion has been made by Hubert Savory, that tweezers may also have been part of the grooming equipment of people in Wales, on the basis of a curved strip of bronze found with urns at Clocaenog in Denbighshire.

Tools for violence

In all previous ages it is possible to excuse the implements which may have served as weapons – flint knives, axes and arrows – as being every day tools which were occasionally turned to more violent ends. These excuses wear thin in this period, when new forms of equipment were made which seem to have no role other than as weapons. Most explicit of all are the halberds which have already been discussed, but the designs of daggers, axe-hammers and barbed arrowheads also carry an inherent threat.

Close combat

Knives and daggers were made from stone and bronze during this period. Flint daggers were only in use at the start of the period covered here and were probably inspired by exquisitely crafted specimens made in Scandinavia. Bronze daggers developed over the centuries from early copper examples hafted with a tang embedded in a wooden or bone handle, to examples hafted by a series of rivets and with ribs serving to reinforce the blade.

No tanged daggers have been found in Wales, although there is no reason to suppose they were not used here, but rivetted daggers are well represented. The earliest radiocarbon-dated example was found in a cist at Candleston Castle in Bridgend, which Jody Deacon and Adam Gwilt have shown was in use between about 2000 and 1950 BC. Another potentially early example was found at Corston Beacon in Pembrokeshire. Analysis of this by Peter Northover suggests that it was made of Irish copper and tin from southwest England, a mix which would favour a casting date before 1900 BC, although it is possible that the smith melted down an old copper tool to make this item at a later date.

Traces of a haft, probably of wood, survived on the Corston Beacon dagger, while fragments of a dagger with the remains of a wooden sheath were also recorded during excavations at St Brides Netherwent in Monmouthshire in 1860, along with part of a whetstone – a reminder that metal blades will have needed sharpening if they were to remain effective. Traces of the hafting arrangements for flint daggers were also preserved on a specimen from a cairn at Ystradfellte in southern Powys which had notches on the side and marks surviving between them, presumably the remains of binding which held haft to blade.

All of these daggers had been buried complete, presumably when they were still in reasonable repair. In other cases the situation seems to have been more complex.

Bone pommels, which once capped the end of dagger hafts, have been found with several cremations in Wales, but in no case have dagger blades been found with them. It is possible that these daggers were dismantled before the pommel was consigned to the flames, but it seems more likely that the blades were gathered up from the ashes after the fire had died down. The living may have thought that the blades would be of more value to them than to the dead.

The name given to many of these blades, 'daggers', contains an assumption that they were linked to violence and this could lead to the conclusion that they were the possessions of men, as was the case with the burial at Corston Beacon

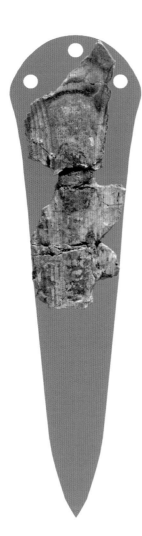

in Pembrokeshire and at many sites elsewhere in Britain. It is hard to be certain in every instance, in part because many of the bone identifications were made in the early years of archaeological study in Wales making their accuracy questionable.

Yet whether wielded by a man or woman, the potential of a dagger to do violence is clear. It was a weapon for the quick and nimble, being used to jab and thrust at an opponent. The wielder of a dagger stood close to their enemy and when their blade pierced flesh, they would have been just inches from their victim. Blood would have been on their hands. The weakness of the weapon was of course that such proximity left the attacker at risk as well – a careless moment would have allowed a skilful opponent to turn the tables with potentially fatal consequences. In contrast, the battle-axe offered the possibility of keeping the fight at arms' length. Mounted on a shaft and swung about the head it would have cleared an arc in front and to the sides of the person who wielded it, dealing crushing blows to anyone foolhardy enough to stand in the way. Its own weakness stemmed from the effort that would have been required to alter the pace or direction of the rhythmic swing, allowing an opponent the possibility of breaking through the guard of the unskilled or distracted – with a dagger thrust perhaps. Dagger and battle-axe may therefore have been complementary, each suited to different types of combat, or perhaps to different stages in a single fight, and while many individuals went to their graves accompanied by one or the other, a few were buried with both.

Death at a distance

Unlike the dagger and the battle-axe, the only long range weapon of this age, the bow and arrow, had been in use in Wales for millennia. The very first, dating back to the Ice Age, are generally interpreted as hunting tools, although by about

Discovery of a battle-axe in a cist at Clap-yr-Arian (central Powys), in 1910.

The axe, which was made from Preseli bluestone, had been placed blade down, as in the photograph.

© The Cambrian Archaeological Association.

Discovery of a battle-axe in a cist at Garthbeibio (northern Powys), in 1923.

© The Cambrian Archaeological Association.

3700 BC they were being used en masse as assault weapons, as demonstrated by the swarm of flint arrowheads around the entrances to enclosures at Carn Brea in Cornwall and Crickley Hill in Gloucestershire. Several arrowheads have also been found embedded in the bones of people who died at this time, demonstrating their effectiveness – and if the people of 3700 BC had realised the potential of the bow and arrow as a weapon there is no reason to believe that either their ancestors or their descendants were unaware of its capacity for violence. The barbed and tanged arrowhead, introduced to Britain around 2400 BC, was an especially vicious design. Its point could puncture flesh with ease while its barbs made it harder for a wounded animal to dislodge, or for an injured adversary to pull out, making a slow death from blood-loss or infection more likely.

There are two sites in Wales where evidence exists for the use of the bow and arrow as a weapon. At Sarn-y-bryn-caled in northern Powys, four burnt arrowheads were found among the cremated remains of an adult, raising the possibility that they

Arrowheads and cremated bone from Sarn-y-bryn-caled (northern Powys).

Were these the arrows that killed the person whose cremated remains can be seen here?

© The National Museum of Wales (Steve Burrow).

Original artefacts housed in the collections of Powysland Museum. (Arrowheads, 4.1cm long).

were the cause of death and were still embedded in the body when it was cremated. In support of this, two arrowheads had lost their tips, probably as a result of their impacting on something hard – the person's bones perhaps; and the remains were found buried at the centre of what is thought to be a ceremonial site. In combination the evidence can be used to weave a story of sacrifice and ritual. At the second site where an individual may have died from arrow wounds, Clocaenog in Denbighshire, eleven burnt arrowheads were found among the cremated bones. Fire damage makes it hard to be certain how many of these had impact fractures, but it is likely that at least three had been damaged in this way. Might this be another case of ritualised killing? Certainly eleven arrows are hard to argue away as a hunting accident.

Of course, counter arguments can be raised in both cases, and there is certainly evidence that arrowheads served a more benign role as grave goods accompanying the dead. This can be clearly seen at Sutton 268' in Glamorgan where seven arrowheads, probably still hafted, had been placed with the body of a man; while an even more impressive collection accompanied cremated remains at Breach Farm in Glamorgan.

Arrowshaft straighteners from Wales.

The groove on these simply shaped stones is designed to hold an unfinished arrowshaft. A single straightener, like that from Eglwysbach (Conwy) can be used as a vice against which the shaft can be bent to help remove any kinks. A pair of straighteners, like those from Breach Farm (Glamorgan) can also be held together around the shaft and used to smooth away any surface blemishes.

© The National Museum of Wales (Steve Burrow, Kevin Thomas).

Original artefacts housed in the collections of Bangor Museum (Eglwysbach), and Amgueddfa Cymru – National Museum Wales (Breach Farm). (Examples from Breach Farm, 5.5cm long).

Many other arrowheads have been excavated from burial mounds, and still more have been found as chance finds in fields, presumably reflecting a general pattern of discard and loss across the landscape. An exceptional concentration was found near Llyn Bugeilyn in northern Powys in the 1920s and 1930s. About thirty arrowheads were discovered during peat cutting, with many others coming to light around the same time. A S Davies recorded his belief that by 1934 over a hundred had been found in total. To these can be added a further dozen found a few kilometres to the south in the 1960s. If these arrowheads were the result of multiple losses during hunting, one could reasonably expect to find similar concentrations in other areas of the uplands where peat has been cut, but this has not been the case. Another explanation must be sought, and the geography of the area may provide an answer, since it contains the source of both the Rivers Wye and Severn, as well as significant feeders for the Dovey Estuary. Hubert Savory suggested that this may have been recognised at this time, leading to the area becoming a focus for some repeated ritual involving archery competitions, or perhaps the burial of archery equipment.

No bows or arrowshafts are known to have been preserved in Wales, leaving the story of archery at this time to rest on arrowheads and stone shaft-straighteners. One other type of artefact may be linked to the subject, although with less certainty. The recoil of a bow string against the inside of the arm can be very painful, and many modern archers wear wristguards to protect themselves against this. Archers from this period would have faced the same problem, and since the middle of the nineteenth century it has been argued that a number of slender perforated stones, sometimes found with burials, were the wristguards of their day. Four 'wristguards' have been found in Wales, one at the medieval site of Llantrithyd in Glamorgan, one from the chamber of a megalithic tomb at Dyffryn Ardudwy in Gwynedd, a third in a hearth at Carneddau 1 in northern Powys, and a final unprovenanced example from Carmarthenshire. The Llantrithyd example was found by members of Cardiff Archaeological Society in a post pit belonging to a later building, and it seems likely that this had disturbed an earlier grave. Hubert Savory who wrote about the piece in the 1970s observed that its form was reminiscent of examples found on the continent rather than in Britain, and more recent work by a team led by Ann Woodward has shown it was made of nephrite, a type of rock which

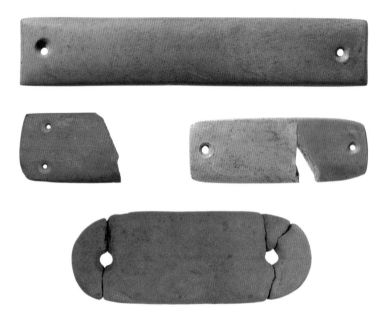

'Wristguards' from Wales.

Clockwise from top: Llantrithyd (Glamorgan), Dyffryn Ardudwy (Gwynedd), Carneddau 1, (northern Powys), and Carmarthenshire.

© National Museum of Wales (Steve Burrow, James Wild).

Original artefacts housed in the collections of Powysland Museum (Carneddau), Carmarthen Museum (Carmarthenshire), and Amgueddfa Cymru – National Museum Wales (others). (Example from Llantrithyd, 13cm long).

is found around the Alps, although other sources are also possible. The design of the Llantrithyd example seems well-suited to its use as a wristguard – it is 13cm long and relatively sturdy; in contrast the examples from Dyffryn Ardudwy and Carmarthenshire are very thin and were found snapped, suggesting they were not designed to withstand rough use. The example from Carneddau 1 is also very short, raising the likelihood that the loosed bow string would have been caught between skin and stone, defeating the purpose of the wristguard.

Given the practical limitations of their design one is left with the problem of suggesting an alternative purpose for these objects. Looking further afield, recent study of 'wristguards' by Ann Woodward's team has confirmed that across Britain there is only a loose correlation between such finds and the discovery of other archery equipment, leading to suggestions that their role may have been symbolic or simply decorative. Such a role would certainly explain the limited practical value of the Welsh examples.

The people revealed

Over the last few chapters, the people of 2400 BC and after have revealed themselves through their material remains as diverse folk. As craftspeople they were potters, stone and bone workers, woodsmen, leatherworkers, makers of textiles and quarrymen. As providers they hunted wild animals, husbanded livestock and tended crops; and at the grave side they reveal themselves as mourners, monument builders and people with a strong sense of ritual and tradition. It could be argued that these were all roles which people had pursued for millennia – tens of millennia in some cases – albeit with variations in the detail of the equipment used and the technological processes that were adopted. For some however, there were new roles.

The miners on the Great Orme, and presumably around other Welsh copper sources, were the first to tunnel deep into the earth. The ore they recovered fuelled the work of smelters and bronze smiths whose alchemy had no precedent. Other people took up weapons of innovative design, and it is tempting to see these halberds, daggers and battle-axes as the badges of people who viewed themselves as warriors. A magpie-like acquisitiveness also reveals itself through a delight in exotic jewellery. The men and women who took part in such work and who cherished these possessions were pioneers in a sense; they endorsed the motifs of a new era, known to archaeologists as The Bronze Age. For most however, the ancient challenges of equipping oneself with everyday tools, providing for the family, maintaining friendships and coping with death must have been far more pressing than the desire to learn new skills or adopt new roles.

Before they died

A population expressive in death, but shy in life – it is a theme which has run through this book, but the contrast seems especially acute in Wales at this time. Over the course of 700 years tens of thousands of people built thousands of barrows, and yet very few traces of their dwelling places survive. The balance of surviving evidence could lead one to believe that these were a gloomy and doom-laden people so obsessed with the end of their lives that they were unwilling to invest in comfort before this moment came. But this cannot be a realistic appraisal of daily life at this time. A useful parallel can be found in the archaeology of ancient Egypt. Here too, burial places proliferate, and settlements are scarce. But in Egypt, tomb paintings survive which show some people who are well-groomed and others dishevelled by work, they show laughter and love as well as sadness. No doubt the people of what is now Wales were similarly diverse but they lived without the benefit of a surviving art tradition which could convey the emotions of their lives and, as in Egypt, they built their homes from short-lived materials while their burial monuments were made from sturdier stuff.

Home

A building excavated at Stackpole Warren in Pembrokeshire in the 1970s provides a rare example of a house from this period. It was four metres in diameter and set in a hollow, with a central hearth, daub-lined wattle walls, probably a conical roof, and an outer porch. There was room within for a small family. The house probably burnt down around 1600 BC, and in the destruction layer were the remains of broken pots, flints, barley grains, animal and human bones. How human bones should have ended up in this collection is not clear, although it is possible that they belonged to the remains of relatives kept with the living.

Another roundhouse of similar size, but this time stone-walled, has been studied by Astrid Caseldine, George Smith and Catherine Griffiths at Llyn Morwynion in Gwynedd. The building began to be covered by peat around 2400 BC; strictly it predates the period covered by this chapter, but other similar structures were found higher up the slopes which might have continued in use. The preservation of pollen in the peat also offered the opportunity to learn about the environment in the area

which, it appears, began to be cleared of woodland when the peat started to form, with animals probably being grazed in the resulting clearings.

In combination Llyn Morwynion and Stackpole Warren show that small, family-sized buildings were current at both the start and end of this period, continuing

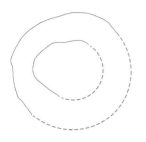 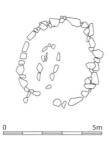 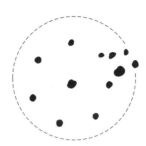

a tradition which was apparent much earlier at sites like Trelystan in northern Powys. Such evidence suggests small groups living in dispersed settlements – no villages have been found in Wales. Indeed the scarcity of surviving houses gives an impression of transience, although this probably reflects the ease with which traces of such structures are destroyed rather than any nomadic instinct among the population as a whole.

The decay of these houses began as soon as their owners abandoned them. Stone and timbers might be reused in other buildings, damp and rot would break down wattle walls and roof thatch, and vegetation would reclaim the land, until all that was visible was an irregular undulation. The ever-improving technology of land clearance and ploughing would soon flatten these out if an area was used by

later generations of arable farmers; or, if the location appealed to later builders, then earth moving projects might remove all traces. Occasional pits below later settlements and fortifications at Moel y Gaer in Flintshire, Bryn Maen Caerau in Ceredigion and Holgan and Pilcornswell Camps, both in Pembrokeshire, may be all that survive of occupation sites which suffered this latter fate. But while houses are scarce, another type of site closely linked to everyday life has survived in some numbers.

Boiling troughs

Thomas Crosbee Cantrill was a geologist employed with the British Geological Survey in South Wales between 1896 and 1909. Cantrill's duties led him to walk large stretches of southwest Wales, as well as parts of Breconshire and Glamorgan, and during his work he took the opportunity to study the ground for evidence of prehistoric occupation. In 1898 he began to notice small heaps of broken and burnt stones at the head of the Tawe Valley, often close to springs. Thanks to Cantrill's work and that of subsequent fieldworkers, over five hundred of these burnt mounds have now been identified in Wales, principally in the west of the country from Pembrokeshire to Anglesey. Not all of them date to the period covered by this book; a few are older, many are more recent, but recent excavation shows that the tradition was well-established in Wales after about 2400 BC. At first Cantrill thought these mounds might cover burials, but their position – often on wet and boggy ground – led him to abandon the idea.

In 1979 and 1981 Dyfed Archaeological Trust undertook the excavation of two of these burnt mounds beside a stream on Rhos Carne Coch ('the moor of the red cairns') in Pembrokeshire. The northern mound was made up of several dumps of burnt stone spread over an area about 13m across and covering three pits dug into a clay subsoil, the largest was probably filled in with burnt stone around 2200 BC. Eighty metres away, the southern mound had a similar composition and also covered three pits. It had been in use for some centuries between 2500 and 1500 BC.

Pits are a common feature at the centre of burnt mounds, and it seems certain they were meant to hold water. At Rhos Carne Coch, the clay subsoil was sufficient to provide a watertight seal, at other sites wooden troughs are also found, sometimes acting as containers, sometimes just preventing the soil from the sides and base of the pit from dirtying the water. For example, at Nant Porth near Bangor a plank-lined trough within a burnt mound was built around 1600 BC and refurbished

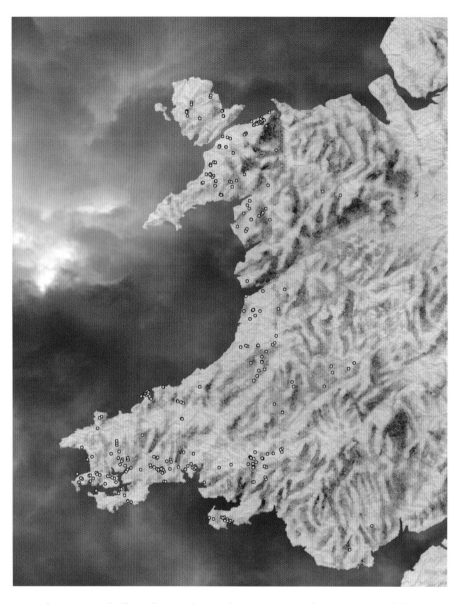

Distribution of burnt mounds in Wales.

Burnt mounds are one of the few types of monument from this period to have a clear regional bias, clustering in the west of the country. It has been argued that they were built away from areas of limestone since this rock, when burnt and added to water, produces caustic slaked lime, but this does not completely explain the distribution. A cultural difference in the way people in east and west Wales heated and used hot water seems more likely.

Based on site data collected by and © Clwyd-Powys Archaeological Trust, Dyfed Archaeological Trust, Glamorgan-Gwent Archaeological Trust and Gwynedd Archaeological Trust; and map data produced by the Ordnance Survey (reproduced with the permission of Ordnance Survey on behalf of The Controller of Her Majesty's Stationery Office, © Crown copyright 2010).

around 1200 BC; a hollowed-out oak tree dating to around 1450 BC served the same purpose in a burnt mound at Herbrandston in Pembrokeshire. The combination of a watertight container, a water supply, and the piles of burnt stone which surround them makes it clear that these were places where hot stones were used to boil water. But why this water was needed remains unclear.

The longest-established theory holds that these were places where food was boiled, and the suitability of these burnt mounds as cooking places has been tested on several occasions, most famously by Michael O'Kelly in Ireland. O'Kelly showed that the water in a 450-litre trough could be brought to the boil in thirty minutes using hot stones, with old stones being fished out as they cooled and new ones added to maintain the temperature. In his experiments, meat wrapped in straw was cooked to perfection, with the straw preventing charcoal and stone splinters from contaminating the meat. Another experiment undertaken at Rhos Carne Coch with a smaller trough demonstrated that around 70kg of stone might have been used for each boiling, meaning that a substantial mound of burnt stone could be accumulated in a relatively small number of cooking sessions. If one accepts the premise that burnt mounds were cooking sites, then the time required for their construction and the quantity of water they could hold make it likely that they were semi-permanent fixtures serving nearby settlements.

One aspect of the evidence from Rhos Carne Coch does not fit neatly into the cooking model. The central part of the northern mound had a large number of stones in a charcoal-stained soil. If these stones had been fished out of a water-filled trough, one would expect them to be clean of charcoal. The cooking theory and the evidence seem to conflict here, as they do at other sites as well. One of the solutions to this problem, first proposed by Laurence Barfield and Mike Hodder, and entertained by Heather James, is that burnt mounds may have been used as saunas, with the stones being heated in a fire and with the water from the trough being poured over them to generate steam inside an overarching tent. In this way, stones and charcoal would remain mixed in the manner seen at Rhos Carne Coch. Good parallels are known for this practice in eastern Europe and north America, but the theory remains unproven in Wales.

All that can be said with absolute certainty is that people at this time seem to have required large quantities of hot water, and pragmatism would suggest that this was useful in more than one part of their lives – for cooking, washing, leather or textile preparation and brewing, to name a few. The benefit of having a structure set up which could deliver this supply, for relatively low effort, versus the prospect of repeatedly boiling small quantities of water over a fire, must have been considerable.

The size of many boiling troughs means that they could have produced more hot water, cooked more food, or brewed more beer than a single family would need, suggesting that they serviced the needs of a wider community. If this was the case,

Gathering at a boiling trough.

© The National Museum of Wales (Tony Daly).

then it is possible that they acted as focal points where people would gather, gossip, and exchange news with their immediate neighbours. The need for such meeting places, whether formal or impromptu, has been a thread running through this book.

Places to meet and celebrate

While boiling troughs probably provided a hub for domestic life when they were in use, other types of sites satisfied the need for a ceremonial focus. In some cases, burial mounds may have fulfilled this role – their summits offering a platform around which the audience might gather – and it is notable that several have been found to contain no burials, as at Brenig 47 in Denbighshire, Great Pale in Carmarthenshire and Six Wells in Glamorgan. Perhaps in these instances it was more important for communities to have a mound which they could use, than it was that they had a monument to their dead.

Still other sites seem purpose-made to serve as arenas, or as open stages for ceremonies. Stone circles are the best known. These sites, with their well-spaced stones, some big some small, have lodged themselves in popular imagination as places of magic and ceremony. Following a custom begun in the seventeenth century many were believed to be the ritual centres of druids – woods of stone to mirror the sacred groves described by the Roman author Tacitus. This erroneous link is preserved in the name 'Druids' Circle' given to a stone circle on Penmaenmawr in Gwynedd. By the middle of the nineteenth century Welsh scholars were stripping away this disinformation, but the assumption that stone circles were, in part, meeting places has remained. Few other explanations fit their form so well.

The classic image of the stone circle is of great stones arranged separately like figures in a coven, all gazing at the centre. Not all are so spectacular, indeed previously unknown circles of small and unimpressive stones continue to be found in low vegetation and out-of-the-way places, but more importantly, the stone circle itself sits at just one end of a spectrum of similar stone, earth and timber monuments.

The Druid's Circle, the archetypal stone circle in Wales, is itself a monument made of composite materials. It consists of about thirty well-spaced stones ranging in height from 1.8m tall to just a few centimetres above the ground. These are the most eye-catching feature of the site, but a low bank of small stones, edged in places

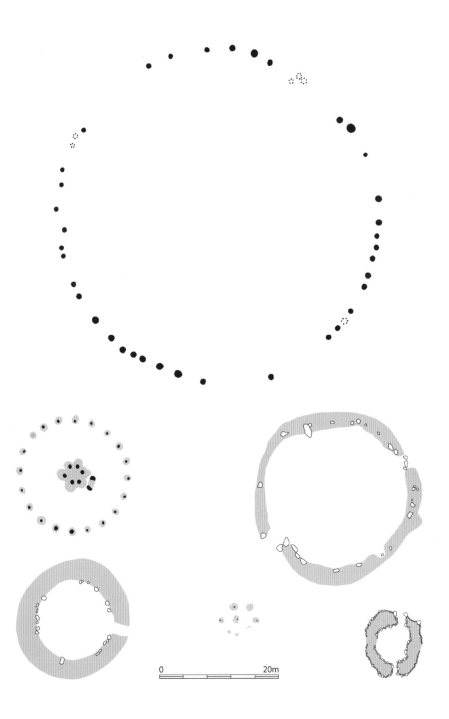

Meeting places were built in different sizes and from a range of materials.

Clockwise from bottom left: embanked stone circle at Letterston 3 (Pembrokeshire); timber circle at Sarn-y-bryn-caled (central Powys); stone circle at Carneddau Hengwm site T (Gwynedd); Druids' Circle (Gwynedd); ring cairn on Cefn Bryn (Gower); pit circle at Yr Allor (Pembrokeshire).

© The National Museum of Wales (Tony Daly).

0   20m

Gors Fawr stone circle (Pembrokeshire), with Preseli Hills on skyline.

© The National Museum of Wales (Steve Burrow).

Druid's Circle (Gwynedd).

© The National Museum of Wales (Steve Burrow).

by a well-built kerb, also survives against the outer face of these upright stones, enclosing the whole with what probably appeared to be a continuous crenellated circuit when first built.

At other sites the stone circle is entirely absent, leaving the encircling bank to enclose the interior on its own. Carn Goch 2 in southern Powys provides an example of these so-called ring cairns. Here local stones, both quarried and gathered from the drift, were set in a neat circle which was to form the inner face of the ring. Further concentric circles were then added beyond this until a thickness of three to four metres had been reached, at which point the outside of the ring was left as a ragged edge. The care with which the inner face of the ring was built, in contrast to the outside, suggests that this site was designed to be appreciated by those who could fit into its limited interior. But there is evidence from other ring cairns that the activities which took place within were not meant to be exclusive to a few. Anthony Ward has argued, on the basis of his work in southwest Wales, that in this area ring cairns tended to be built in locations where they could be overlooked. This

suggests that those not privileged enough to stand within the circle itself viewed events from adjacent high ground.

Stone circles and ring cairns are durable markers in the landscape. Other meeting places decayed more quickly, only to be discovered by chance during excavations, or as a result of aerial photography. The best known example in Wales is Sarn-y-bryn-caled in northern Powys, a circle of timbers discovered through aerial photography by J K St Joseph and dated through excavation by Alex Gibson to around 2100 BC. The outer circle consisted of twenty posts, each one possibly rising more than 3m high in a circle 17.5m in diameter, with an entrance in the southwest side. Within this was another circle of six posts, about 3m in diameter, with two more set beside them. In total the excavator estimated that it would have taken around 3,224 man-hours to build the site.

The size of the host

While the Sarn-y-bryn-caled timber circle was a substantial structure which could have held many people inside, other much smaller sites are known. Circles about 7m in diameter have

been identified at Pantymenyn and Yr Allor in Pembrokeshire, although later use of these sites makes their original form impossible to prove. An even smaller space was enclosed at Pont ar Daf in the Brecon Beacons, where a wall of timbers set in a 3m diameter bedding trench was built between 1900 and 1750 BC. The small size of these circles suggests that they were meeting places for the few, although it is possible that many more could have gathered to play a part in proceedings from outside.

The ring cairn at Cefn Caer Euni 2 in Gwynedd was also small, with an interior space less than 4m in diameter. In southwest Wales, Anthony Ward has shown that ring cairns generally enclosed a space between eight and fifteen metres across. Stone circles of a similar size are also known, but so are larger examples. O G S Crawford excavated two circles in Gwynedd, a 53m diameter stone circle – the largest in Wales – at Carneddau Hengwm, site T, and a 37m diameter earthen circle, site S, 25m to the north. Such sites could have held a great many people although this is not proof in itself that they ever did so.

In combination therefore it seems that meeting places of different designs and capacities were being built across Wales during this period. As in previous ages, the decision as to whether to build with stone monoliths, rocks, earth, or timber was probably influenced by many factors: the availability of raw materials, the building traditions current in a locality, and the nature of the ceremony to be conducted at the meeting place. Of these, and other reasons, it is the nature of the ceremony which is of pivotal concern and on which one would expect excavation to shed most light, but not all functions for a meeting place would have left evidence in the ground.

Strange ceremonies

Commemoration, celebration, negotiation and exchange may all have taken place at and around stone and timber circles, and ring cairns, without leaving any trace at all. Other activities might leave more for archaeologists to pick over, but often those traces are not easy to interpret. The example of the two timber circles discovered off the coast of Norfolk in the late 1990s provides a clear example of the problem. The most extensively examined of these, known as Seahenge, was in a remarkable state of preservation, allowing one a good sense of the monument's original form.

Seahenge consisted of a wall of split timbers, 7m in diameter, entered by a fork in one of the posts. In the centre was an upturned oak tree, its roots free, like branches in the air. An enormous amount has been learnt through the study of this rare survivor. It was built in a salt-marsh in the spring or early summer of 2049 BC, its timbers were felled and worked with at least fifty-one bronze axes, the central timber was secured with a rope made from honeysuckle, and the circle was orientated with reference to the solstices. But the only clue to the purpose of the monument itself is the upturned tree at its centre. Perhaps this had a clear meaning for its builders, or perhaps it was meant to be a mystery – a statement that the visitor had entered a strange space where the normal rules of life did not apply. Certainly it suggests a place where symbolism and difference were important.

It is likely that some meeting places in Wales were used to evoke similar feelings among the population, and in this regard one discovery in the circle at Pantymenyn is of particular interest. Here, in a pit, were found remains of henbane, a poisonous narcotic associated with hallucinations, among other symptoms. It is not a substance which is likely to have been regularly used and if its presence at Pantymenyn was deliberate then it suggests that visitors to this circle were more interested in accessing other worlds, than they were in discussing the mundane affairs of this one.

It also seems that the remains of the dead were used to make special the experience of visiting some circles. For example at Letterston 3 cremated bone was placed in the entrance to the circle, perhaps to sanctify the space, a practice already noted at other sites in previous centuries. Having passed through to the interior, the only evidence that the users of the circle left behind were traces of burning on some of the quartz paving that floored the interior – fire was a part of their ritual, but it is not known what role this served.

Death and fire are important themes at another site, Brenig 44 in Denbighshire, a ring cairn with a timber circle set inside its bank. Cremated remains were found both in the centre of the circle, and in a pit dug against the inner face of the ring, while across the site were found a number of pits which contained only charcoal. These, argues the excavator Frances Lynch, reflect the real function of the site, while the burials were of only secondary importance to its users.

The burial of token quantities of human bone is a recurrent theme at other ring cairns and seems to have been taken to an extreme at Aber Camddwr in Ceredigion. At the centre of this circle was buried an urn which contained no human bone at all, suggesting the presence of the dead in spirit if not in practice. Interestingly, a stake had been driven through this urn some time after it was buried, suggesting that it may have been ritually killed, or perhaps more prosaically that its location had been forgotten. The ring cairn at Aber Camddwr also had another link with

death. In a pit not far from the urn were found the badly cremated remains of a headless child set on an oak plank. To the excavator, A H A Hogg, this was evidence of a dedicatory sacrifice, but there is no proof that the child died an unnatural death, and it is possible that the head was removed as part of the mortuary ritual.

Sacrifice at meeting places like these is a popular theme in contemporary imagination. One of the upright stones in the Druids' Circle has a hollow in its face and local tradition maintained that this was where the bodies of infants were placed after sacrifice. Excavation by W E Griffiths in the 1950s did indeed find the burials of adolescents at this site, but the span of time involved leaves no possibility that modern storytelling reflects the actual circumstances of their deaths. The evidence is stronger at the Sarn-y-bryn-caled timber circle where, as already described, four arrowheads were found mixed with the cremated remains of an adult in a pit at the centre of the monument. This evidence for sacrifice is persuasive, if not conclusive. As stone circle expert Aubrey Burl has argued, today's visitor to a stone circle:

> may be standing not in a scientific observatory or contemplative chapel but in a macabre enclosure of death where people, fearful in a precarious world, offered fire and human beings in return for their own safe-keeping.

Moel Goedog 1 (Gwynedd).

This ring cairn is set just north of a trackway that skirts the flanks of the mountain; it is likely that this route was in use when the circle was built.

© National Museum of Wales (Steve Burrow).

Calling an end to the meeting

Meeting places of earth and stone could have served their purpose for hundreds of years; structurally their design was sound, and radiocarbon dates from Brenig 44 in Denbighshire have shown that in this instance at least, a meeting place was returned to over several generations. Many other meeting places would not have lasted so long. Timber circles would have shown signs of decay within years of their construction, requiring continuing repair if they were to survive across the generations. Other sites, particularly ring cairns, seem to have been deliberately slighted.

Several examples can be offered of this practice. A number of cremation deposits were buried inside the ring cairn at Moel Goedog 1 in Gwynedd, both during and after its construction. One was set in a pit so shallow that its protecting urn would have protruded above ground level. Rain and frost would have soon destroyed this pot, but its preservation was assured by the prompt infilling of the interior of the circle with a layer of stones. This effectively prevented any further use of the circle as an area for ceremony. A similar infilling took place at Carn Goch 2 in southern Powys, where new stone was probably brought to the site for this purpose rather than simply being acquired through the demolition of the circle itself. At Letterston 3 in Pembrokeshire and Pond Cairn in Bridgend, stacks of turf were used to infill their open interiors, converting them into mounds.

Brenig ring cairn with the burial mound known as Boncyn Arian beyond. Both sites were reconstructed following excavation and now form part of the Brenig Archaeological Trail in Denbighshire.

It is not unusual for barrows and meeting places to be built close together. At Cefn Caer Euni (Gwynedd), a kerb circle was built a few paces from a ring cairn. At Mynydd Epynt (southern Powys), a burial mound was raised just 50m from a stone circle. In some areas, for example, on Cefn Bryn (Gower) and Penmaenmawr (Conwy), there are multiple examples of burial mounds interspersed with meeting places.

© The National Museum of Wales (Steve Burrow).

Whether this obsolescence was seen as a natural development of these sites, anticipated from the outset, or whether it was a traumatic decision for the communities involved is not known. On Cefn Bryn on Gower, however, the presence of seven ring cairns built in close proximity suggests that some communities did not object to the labour involved in replacing their meeting places periodically.

Meeting with whom?

It is likely that some stone, timber and earth circles will have been built just to satisfy the needs of a local population, but even quite modest-sized circles seem to have drawn people from further afield, as evidence from Great Carn ring cairn 1 on Cefn Bryn and Moel Goedog 1 in Gwynedd demonstrates. At the first of these sites, around 1700 BC, a pit was dug near the centre of the circle and some soil containing less than a gram of cremated bone was placed within it. Curiously, the soil does not match that of the surrounding area, suggesting that someone had dug up a burial site elsewhere and brought some of its earth to link their own land with this place. A similar sequence of events took place at Moel Goedog 1, but in neither case is it known how far these remains were carried.

In the case of the larger stone circles it is tempting to imagine them as gathering places for communities who lived over a wide area, all drawn together for annual festivals, but this need not be the case, since size of circle need not have been an indicator of regional importance. A stronger case for regional importance can be made for those circles which were set on routeways, perhaps linking communities dozens of kilometres apart.

Travelling through Wales

After thousands of years of human life in Wales there is no doubt that all corners of the country will have been explored, and all feasible routes across the land mapped, if only in the mind. Not all routes would have been equal: local politics may have meant that some paths were best avoided, dense vegetation will have made navigation of others difficult, and marshy ground will have made for heavy going. Most important of all, the lie of the land would have channelled movement. River valleys have been exploited for millennia and they continue to provide the outline for much of the road network across Wales. Since the country was still extensively wooded in this period, it may have been easier for travellers to keep sight of guiding landmarks if they walked in the uplands. The mountain walker may have benefited from another advantage; here the possibility of trespass would have been less than in the more fertile lowlands.

Once the shortest, safest path between two areas had been discovered, the same route was probably followed across the generations, keeping the vegetation low and encouraging others to follow and settlement to accumulate. As there are no unequivocal road surfaces dating from this period, the best guide to the existence of a former routeway is probably the presence of monuments running along appropriate topography. The circle of stones on Mynydd Epynt in southern Powys provides an example of this. Built on a mountain saddle it is a natural assumption that people from the valleys on either side met here. Indeed the excavator G C Dunning suggested that two gaps in the circle may mark the path of a former trackway between the two. Whether Dunning was correct in this interpretation or not, there can be no doubt that many short tracks of this sort were maintained across Wales, linking communities with water sources, crops, pasture and neighbours.

Standing stone at Llanbedr (Gwynedd).

Set beside the mouth of the Afon Artro, this stone may have been raised to mark a safe harbour for mariners.

© The National Museum of Wales (Steve Burrow).

A longer trackway has been postulated across Penmaenmawr, linking the coastlands east of Bangor and the valley of the River Conwy, while avoiding the precipitous coastline around the flanks of the mountain. A number of the circles and burial mounds on Penmaenmawr cluster in a line along this 'short-cut', suggesting that they were built to be seen by passers-by, and the largest of all, the Druids' Circle is flattened on its northern side, as though it had been built around a trackway that was already in existence. Today the route has been formalised as the North Wales Path. W E Griffiths, the first to suggest that this concentration of monuments marked the line of an early track, argued that it had been used by men trading Irish copper into the interior of Britain. Certainly this event must have happened, although whether it was along this particular path cannot be known.

Other tracks have been postulated in the borderlands of Montgomeryshire and Shropshire, where a number of long east-west hills provide ridgeways linking the interior of Wales with the English lowlands. Such ridgeways continued to be important until quite recent times; as H N Jerman noted, in the nineteenth century they provided a means of driving cattle to market while avoiding the toll booths that controlled the roads in the lowlands. The concentration of monuments along the Kerry Ridgeway is less pronounced than at Penmaenmawr, with the Two Tumps barrows at its western end providing the most obvious marker and a scatter of stone circles and other burial mounds peppering its length. Even so the logic of its use is clear and the discovery of flint nodules from southern or eastern England at Cloddiau, just north of Kerry, suggests that the ridgeway may have been just one stage in a far more extensive network of paths.

E G Bowen and C A Gresham identified two other likely routes in southern Gwynedd, linking the west coast with the adjacent uplands. These differ from those described above in that parts of their length are marked by isolated standing stones, rather than by barrows or scatters of lost artefacts. The start of one trackway is suggested by a very large standing stone beside the tidal mark of the River Artro at Llanbedr. From here the route climbs north along the flanks of the Rhinog Mountains; following the contours of the mountains it turns east along the hillside that flanks the Glaslyn Estuary, passing the circle and cairn at Moel Goedog on its way. After a couple of hours walking along a less well-defined section of the route the traveller enters a long wide valley, its end marked by the jagged crown of the cairn on Bryn Cader Faner, from which the route descends to Trawsfynydd.

Cairn at Bryn Cader Faner (Gwynedd), looking southwest along a natural route across Moel Ysgyfarnogod.

The projecting 'crown' of slabs has been forced outwards by the weight of the cairn.

© The National Museum of Wales (Steve Burrow).

Stone markers

The standing stones, tall upright monoliths, along the western half of the southern Gwynedd paths serve a recognisable role as way markers, useful for modern as well as ancient travellers; and the possibility that many other stones across Wales served a similar purpose has been a recurrent theme in discussion of these monuments. Several scholars have noted that many are positioned near watercourses, suggesting that they may have served to direct travellers to, or along, streams or rivers. In the uplands, standing stones, whether erected singly or in short lines are sometimes found on passes, suggesting a role in directing travellers.

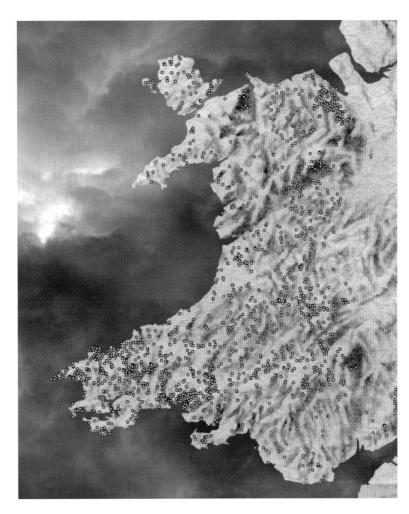

Distribution of standing stones in Wales.

Based on site data collected by and © Clwyd-Powys Archaeological Trust, Dyfed Archaeological Trust, Glamorgan-Gwent Archaeological Trust and Gwynedd Archaeological Trust; and map data produced by the Ordnance Survey (reproduced with the permission of Ordnance Survey on behalf of The Controller of Her Majesty's Stationery Office, © Crown copyright 2010).

With over 900 standing stones probably dating from this period it would be surprising if all were way markers. In 1875 E L Barnwell listed all the possible functions for standing stones which his imagination, and evidence, would support. Some he knew from excavation evidence marked burials, others he thought might commemorate the location of a battle or of sacrifices, still others might have been worshipped in their own right. Most importantly he noted that many may have been valued for different reasons at different times.

Certainly some standing stones mark places of long-standing interest, with several apparently being erected over earlier pits, hinting at the renewal of wooden markers. The inclusion of token quantities of human bone below a standing stone excavated at Bridgend also suggests that in this instance, those who raised the stone wanted to add gravitas to the moment. Other standing stones did not themselves cover burials but instead provided an additional marker on burial mounds, for example at Tyddyn Bach in Gwynedd and Linney Burrows in Pembrokeshire, while an earlier stone protruded through the burial mound at Bedd Branwen on Anglesey.

In cases such as these, the likely function of the standing stone can only be gleaned with reference to other elements of the site both around and below it – cairns, pits and human remains – and this is a useful cautionary note in the interpretation of unexcavated examples. In some cases, a standing stone might be the sole survivor of a stone row or circle, as has been argued, controversially, and ultimately unconvincingly, for the massive stone in the church wall at Ysbyty Cynfyn in Ceredigion. In other cases, as at Mynydd Llangyndeyrn 1 in Carmarthenshire, and Stackpole Warren in Pembrokeshire the standing stone might be all that is visible of a more complex clustering of pits and posts which mark the activities that occurred around the stone.

Standing stone at Maen Llia (southern Powys).

© Steve Burrow.

Standing stones, like stone circles, cairns and other burial mounds have long attracted attention and speculation. Massive and unyielding across the centuries they exert a powerful appeal to people from all walks of life. For some their attraction stems from the link they offer to a past of wished-for earth mysteries: they are a magnet for diverse beliefs in ley lines and energy foci, and some have become places of pagan ceremonies; a few are even places of pilgrimage. The varied ways in which these ancient sites are used are a testament to their power to stir the spirit.

Leaving the Shadowland

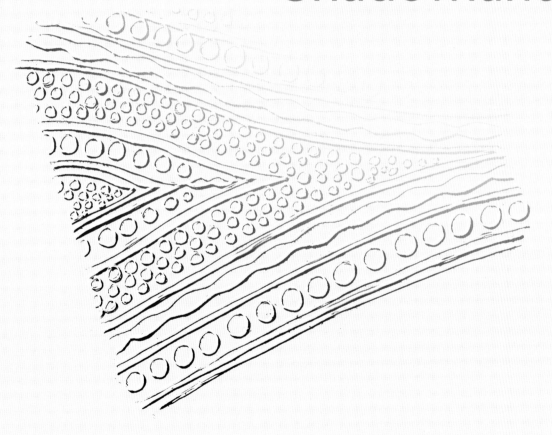

At the start of the period covered here the fuels for this narrative – the sites and artefacts – were few and far-between; at its end they are overwhelming in number. More importantly, in the later centuries covered here, these remains are found in all parts of the country. The picture produced is sometimes sketchy but it is truly national in its extent – there is no need to extrapolate evidence from a burial in the north when attempting to comment on life in the south, or vice versa.

This truly national picture is revealing for its conformity. Across the country, people made similar items, built similar types of sites, and then used them in similar ways. The overall impression is of values shared between communities, something which may have made it easier for neighbours to maintain necessary friendships. Such relationships may have been a matter of life and death in times of famine or other hardship.

This common culture extended beyond the modern national boundaries and is recognisable across much of Britain and Ireland. Indeed a visitor entering Wales from what are now northern Britain, western England or Ireland would probably have recognised the burial mounds, stone circles and standing stones for what they were. They could have picked up an axe head made locally and known how to haft it from long familiarity with those in use in their own regions. Less familiar would have been the mines and the smelting sites associated with them – these were probably specific to the places in western Britain where these minerals occurred. Yet with the exception of the specific tools of their trade – such as stone mauls and bone digging tools – the cultural debris in these mining regions was not markedly different from that found in any other area.

Leaving aside accidents of geography and geology there are few grounds upon which to hang a belief in Wales as possessing a culture distinct from that of its neighbours in England and Ireland. Sometimes it seems that people enjoyed a close connection with communities beyond the modern borders, as implied by the early adoption in Wales of Irish copper and later on, as Frances Lynch has noted, by the adoption in North Wales of aspects of burial rites, monument style and pot designs common in northern England.

Like cultural differences, social hierarchies are also hard to identify in Wales in this period; society seems better characterised as a cultural commonwealth than as a land of princes and chieftains. A few individuals were buried with great wealth, but these were exceptions, and the burial places around them rarely suggest that they were members of powerful and long-lived dynasties. In general the evidence points to small communities facing similar problems in similar ways. Indeed, it is hard to imagine how the uniformity of this time could have given rise to the confused variety of the modern world, but the seeds of change were present in the historical path which this book has described, and by 1500 BC they had germinated.

Whereas prior to 1500 BC the people who inhabited Wales seem for the most part strange and remote, their motivations obscure and often morbid, after this date the archaeological record changes radically: away with death, and in its place a celebration of life in all its mundane glory. And as the years pass, those themes, familiar to modern minds, which have their origins in the shadowland became ever more apparent and persuasive: the need to defend one's possessions, and the urge to acquire more.

Funerals continued to play a part for a time, with just a few rough boulder-built cairns being built beside the earlier burial mounds, and with cemeteries such as Capel Eithin on Anglesey still being used. But after a few centuries the dead become as invisible to archaeologists as they were around 3000 BC, not to reappear in any numbers until the occupation of Wales by the Romans.

In place of their role as mourners at burial mounds and participants in unknown rituals, people reveal themselves as farmers and home builders. Field systems begin to appear, immortalising the protagonists who took on the first of these roles. The most comprehensively studied in Wales is that on St David's Head in Pembrokeshire where the landscape was divided into long strips running perpendicular to the crest of Carn Llidi, probably sometime after about 1400 BC. Some of these boundaries have formed the basis of the modern field divisions in the area, the old world determining the shape of the new. Another series of field walls on Mynydd Llangynderyn in Carmarthenshire probably predates 1000 BC. For the first time, parts of Wales were clearly owned and obviously marked for specific purposes: stock control and arable farming. The intensity of this arable farming in some parts of western Britain led to soil erosion on such a scale that the rivers which flow to the east of Wales are now lined with thick layers of alluvium.

In the years after 1500 BC, people also made their settlements more sturdy and in consequence easier for archaeologists to find. This trend began slowly, but within a thousand years large numbers of small lightly enclosed farmsteads had been built. These field systems and farmsteads suggest that demarcation and ownership of the land had become dominant themes in a way that would probably have been foreign in the Wales of 3000–1500 BC. Before 1500 BC the land was marked out for the generations of the dead; after, it was arranged as a resource for the living, and such displays of ownership were not restricted to land. The hoards of metal goods which were buried after 1500 BC vastly outnumber those which were buried before and, doubtless, ownership and acquisitiveness will have increased the likelihood of disputes. The continued development of weapons may not be coincidental to this. The dagger, once a pre-eminent symbol of power, was made longer, offering its owner more reach to thrust the point, and then strengthened, giving the power to slash at an enemy. The making of spears extended the distance between combatants still further. Shields become more common around this time, presumably in response.

Around 800 BC, the tops of hills began to be fortified, with early examples in this area including structures on top of The Breiddin and at Moel y Gaer, Dinorben, Llwyn Bryn-dinas, and Beeston Castle. Some were probably permanently settled, others may only have been occupied when the surrounding population feared attack. Whether such attacks were regular, or whether these high places were as much about an elite displaying their power, the evidence suggests that the threat of violence had become a powerful motivator. But the response to this threat was not uniform across the country. Large hillforts dominate the Welsh marches, but are rare in west Wales where small defended enclosures are more common. Eight hundred years on, when the Romans reached Wales, they described it as being occupied by four tribes: Demetae and Silures in the south, Deceangli and Ordovices in the north – a divided land, in contrast to the apparent uniformity of the evidence for the years 3000–1500 BC.

These Roman conquerors would have seen many of the sites recorded in this book, and most probably survived in far better condition than they do today. But millennia-old stone circles, barrows, henges and standing stones will have been even more incomprehensible to them than they are to us, benefiting as we do from centuries of study. Instead, the living land the Romans occupied was probably largely familiar as a place of fields and farmsteads, while the people they subjugated were best characterised as farmers and warriors rather than mound builders and shadow-folk. Wales had come a long way since 3000 BC.

Further reading

The literature relating to this period is too vast to reference every article that has inspired this book. Instead, what follows are details of those subject overviews and key reports which can provide a basis for further exploration of the subject. Examination of the bibliographies they contain will provide the additional detail which lack of space precludes here. For those who want more immediate access to the main sources, three main journals have provided a regular outlet for key papers on this period. *Archaeologia Cambrensis*, *Archaeology in Wales*, and to a lesser extent *The Proceedings of the Prehistoric Society*. The excellent indexes to *Archaeologia Cambrensis* will be of particular use in identifying articles relevant to specific sites or subjects. For details of ongoing projects and of relevant sites within Wales, see the websites and databases managed by Wales's four regional archaeological trusts: Glamorgan-Gwent Archaeological Trust, Dyfed Archaeological Trust, Clwyd-Powys Archaeological Trust and Gwynedd Archaeological Trust. In addition, most of the material remains discussed here are stored in collections held by museums in Wales, with (at the time of writing) key displays being open to the public at *Amgueddfa Genedlaethol Caerdydd - National Museum Cardiff*, *Bangor, Wrexham, Powysland Museum* and *Oriel Ynys Môn* on Anglesey. Finally, Cadw has published an excellent series of regional guides for those wishing to visit sites from this period, although some are now difficult to obtain.

The remainder of this bibliography is arranged according to the chapter structure of the main text with titles being abbreviated in some cases.

Introduction (pp 1–4)

The very early history of Wales falls outside the scope of this book, but for a general introduction see F M Lynch, S Aldhouse-Green and J L Davies's *Prehistoric Wales* (Sutton, 2000), while my book *The tomb builders in Wales 4000–3000 BC* (Amgueddfa Cymru - National Museum Wales, 2006) provides a prequel to this volume.

The years around 3000 BC (pp 7–32)

The main sources of information about Wales's passage tombs can be found in W J Hemp's 'The chambered cairn of Bryn Celli Ddu' (*Archaeologia*, volume 80, 1930), with a reinterpretation being offered by S Burrow's 'Bryn Celli Ddu: alignment, construction, date and ritual' (*Proceedings of the Prehistoric Society*, volume 76, 2010). T G E Powell and G E Daniel's *Barclodiad y Gawres* (Liverpool University Press, 1956) describes work at this other great site.

The results of the pivotal excavations at Llandegai are published in F M Lynch and C Musson's 'A prehistoric and early medieval complex at Llandegai, near Bangor, North Wales' (*Archaeologia Cambrensis*, volume 150, 2001). The results of further important excavations adjacent to Llandegai site await publication in the same journal. Evidence relating to other circular enclosures presumed to be of the same date is summarised in S Burrow's article in J Leary, T Darvill and D Field's *Round mounds and monumentality in the British Neolithic and beyond* (Oxbow Books, 2010).

Key sources relating to finds of human remains at ceremonial sites include the Llandegai report noted above and A Gibson's 'Excavations at the Sarn-y-bryn-caled cursus complex, Welshpool, Powys' (*Proceedings of the Prehistoric Society*, volume 60, 1994). Burials proper from this period tend to be published along with other discoveries at the same sites. For example, W J Britnell's 'The excavation of two round barrows at Trelystan, Powys' (*Proceedings of the Prehistoric Society*, volume 48, 1982), W Warrilow, G Owen and W J Britnell's 'Eight ring-ditches at Four Crosses, Llandysilio, Powys' (*Proceedings of the Prehistoric Society*, volume 52, 1986). The Gop Cave evidence appears in W Boyd Dawkins's 'The cairn and sepulchral cave at Gop, near Prestatyn' (*Archaeological Journal*, volume 58, 1901).

The core evidence from the Walton Basin is published in A Gibson's *The Walton Basin Project* (Council for British Archaeology, 1999), although work has continued in the area since this was published. More information about the contemporary pottery discovered at this site can be found in A Gibson's article in I Kinnes and G Varndell's '*Unbaked urns of rudely shape': essays on British and Irish pottery for Ian Longworth* (Oxbow Books, 1995).

S H Warren's 'Excavations at the Stone-Axe factory of Graig-Lwyd, Penmaenmawr' (*Journal of the Royal Anthropological Institute*, 1921) details the original work undertaken at this axe production site. Further work is described in J Ll Williams and A Davidson's 'Survey and excavation at the Graiglwyd Neolithic axe factory, Penmaenmawr' (*Archaeology in Wales*, volume 38, 1998). The importance of this site for the wider stone axe 'trade' can be gleaned from T H M Clough and W A Cummins's *Stone axe studies, volume 2* (Council for British Archaeology, 1988), while R J Bradley and M Edmonds's *Interpreting the axe trade* (Cambridge University Press, 1993) presents a narrative view of the evidence. The story of the Monkton up Wimborne burials is discussed in M Green's *A landscape revealed* (Tempus Publishing, 2000). An introduction to the other stone tools from this and later periods can be found in M Edmonds's *Stone tools and society* (Batsford, 1995). Mace heads and belt-sliders are discussed in F E S Roe and I McInnes's articles in J M Coles and D D A Simpson's, *Studies in ancient Europe* (Leicester University Press, 1968). Final publication of Ogmore-by-Sea is still awaited, but results are summarised in M Hamilton and S Aldhouse-Green's 'Ogmore-by-Sea' (*Archaeology in Wales*, volume 39, 1999).

Turning to the more ephemeral traces of human impact in Wales, A E Caseldine's *Environmental archaeology in Wales* (Saint David's University College, 1990) remains the most recent summary of the evidence. A G Smith and E W Cloutman's 'Reconstruction of Holocene vegetation history at Waun-Fignen-Felen, an upland site in south Wales'

(*Philosophical Transactions of the Royal Society of London*, volume B322, 1988), demonstrates how much can be achieved with pollen data, and A E Caseldine and C Earwood's 'A Neolithic wetland site at Abercynafon, Talybont, south Wales' (*Journal of Wetland Archaeology*, volume 4, 2004), describes a rare example of preserved wood from this time period

2900–2500 BC. An insular folk (pp 33–52)

A good narrative introducing the European evidence can be found in A W R Whittle's *Europe in the Neolithic* (Cambridge University Press, 1996) and R J Harrison's *The Beaker folk* (Thames and Hudson, 1980), with the substance of more recent debates on the origins of Beaker use and its relationship to other cultural traditions appearing in articles within F Nicolis's *Bell Beakers today* (Provincia Autonoma di Trento, 2001). Turning to the Welsh evidence Gibson's *Walton Basin* and Britnell's *Trelystan* continue to be key sources throughout this chapter. Both are referenced above.

Grooved Ware pottery is well covered in R Cleal and A MacSween's *Grooved Ware in Britain and Ireland* (Oxbow Books, 1999). A broader discussion of how the art style of passage tombs began to be used on pottery can be found in R J Bradley's 'Death and entrances: a contextual analysis of megalithic art' (*Current Anthropology*, volume 30, 1989).

A good summary of the British and Irish evidence for houses in this period can be found throughout T C Darvill and J S Thomas's *Neolithic houses in northwest Europe and beyond* (Oxbow Books, 1996). M Parker Pearson's work at Durrington Walls is still ongoing but a summary of the settlement evidence is published in M Larsson and M Parker Pearson's *From Stonehenge to the Baltic* (British Archaeological Reports, 2007).

J Harding's *Henge monuments of the British Isles* (Tempus, 2003) provides an introduction to the subject of ceremonial sites from this period, and works well in combination with the added site detail provided by A F Harding and G E Lee's *Henge monuments and related sites of Great Britain* (British Archaeological Reports, 1987). Excepting Llandegai which is referenced above, references to other henges in Wales can be found in the next section.

In addition to Edmonds's *Stone tools and society*, referenced above, an overview of much of the relevant stone work from this period in Wales can be found in my book *Catalogue of the Mesolithic and Neolithic collections in the National Museums & Galleries of Wales* (National Museums & Galleries of Wales, 2003).

Gibson's Walton Basin report covers the evidence for large scale enclosures in Wales, with added comparative material being published in Gibson's article in A Gibson and D D A Simpson's, *Prehistoric ritual and religion* (Sutton Publishing, 1998).

Stonehenge remains the most intensively studied, and hotly debated site covered by this book. For a detailed review of the excavation evidence see R M J Cleal, K E Walker and R Montague's *Stonehenge in its landscape* (English Heritage, 1995), although twenty-first century work is currently superseding this. Ongoing work in the Preseli Hills is summarised in recent issues of *Archaeology in Wales* (2002 to present). The question of how the bluestones reached Stonehenge has a literature of its own. H H Thomas's original report on the subject 'The source of the stones of Stonehenge' (*The Antiquaries Journal*, volume 3, 1923) is well worth revisiting, as is R J C Atkinson *Stonehenge* (Thomas Hamilton, 1956) for discussion of the possible route the stones took. The major sources in support of glacial transportation are G A Kellaway 'Glaciation and the stones of Stonehenge' (*Nature*, volume 233, 1971), and R S Thorpe, O Williams-Thorpe, D G Jenkins and J S Watson 'The geological sources and transport of the bluestones of Stonehenge, Wiltshire, UK' (*Proceedings of the Prehistoric Society*, volume 57:2, 1991).

2400 BC and after. Bowing to the habits of foreigners (pp 53–80)

The characterisation of metals and their attribution to specific source deposits is a field which continues to evolve. For a now-dated overview of Northover's work see his paper in H N Savory's *Guide catalogue to the Bronze Age collections* (National Museum of Wales, 1980). Recent developments in the application of lead isotope analysis to this subject are covered in B Rohl and S Needham's *The circulation of metal in the British Bronze Age* (British Museum Press, 1998). W O'Brien's *Ross Island* (National University of Ireland, 2004) provides detailed discussion of the most significant copper source for this time.

Examples of copper and subsequent tool types are published in Savory's *Guide catalogue* (cited above). Useful discussion of halberds can be found in R O'Flaherty's 'A weapon of choice – experiments with a replica Irish Early Bronze Age halberd' (*Antiquity*, volume 81, 2007). The chronology of British metalwork is summarised in S Needham's 'Chronology and periodisation in the British Bronze Age' (*Acta Archaeologica*, volume 67, 1996).

Evidence for early activity at Welsh mines has been regularly published in *Archaeology in Wales* since 1987 thanks to S Timberlake and his colleagues in the Early Mines Research Group, reports including particularly early dates were published in 2004 and 2006. More substantial reports include S Timberlake's *Excavations on Copa Hill, Cwmystwyth* (British Archaeological Reports, 2003) and S Timberlake and A J N W Prag's *The archaeology of Alderley Edge* (British Archaeological Reports, 2005). A flavour of experimental work which has attempted to replicate early smelting technology can be found in the above volumes and in O'Brien's *Ross Island* (already cited). The quote from G Plattes comes from *A discovery of subterraneal treasure* (1653).

Britain and Ireland's earliest gold objects are described in G Eogan's *The accomplished art* (Oxbow Monograph 42, 1994). For discussion of the process by which gold was transformed from worthless material to valued metal, see C Renfrew's *Prehistory* (Weidenfeld & Nicholson, 2007). Wales's earliest gold object is discussed in S Timberlake, A Gwilt and M Davis's 'A copper Age / Early Bronze Age gold disc from Banc Tynddol' (*Antiquity*, volume 78, 2004).

D L Clarke's *Beaker pottery of Great Britain and Ireland* (Cambridge University Press, 1970) remains the standard text for Beaker's in Wales, although many others have been discovered since. Lynch's paper in Lynch et al's *Prehistoric Wales* (cited above) provides a more recent summary of the Welsh evidence. References to many of the sites discussed in this book can be found here.

The 'Bill Sikes' quote comes from J Abercromby's *A study of the Bronze Age pottery of Great Britain and Ireland and its associated grave goods* (Clarendon Press, 1912). But a more measured discussion of the question of population replacement at this time can be found in N Brodie's *The Neolithic - Bronze Age transition in Britain* (British Archaeological Reports, 1994). The Amesbury Archer and Boscombe Bowmen are published in A Fitzpatrick's *The Amesbury Archer and the Boscombe Bowmen* (Trust for Wessex Archaeology, 2011), although several useful summaries of discoveries can be found online. In addition, M Parker Pearson and others are currently carrying out a major study looking at human remains from this period in Britain, interim results have been published in Larsson and Parker Pearson's *From Stonehenge to the Baltic* (cited above).

The abandonment of Grooved Ware is discussed in Cleal and MacSween's *Grooved Ware* (cited above), while the continued use of henges in Wales is discussed in A Gibson's 'Excavation and survey at Dyffryn Lane henge complex' (*Proceedings of the Prehistoric Society*, volume 76, 2010). The start of Beaker usage in Britain continues to be actively researched: see articles in Larsson and Parker Pearson's *From Stonehenge to the Baltic* (cited above) and S Needham's 'Transforming Beaker culture in north-west Europe' (*Proceedings of the Prehistoric Society*, volume 71, 2005).

Many Beaker burials have been found in Wales, with a flavour of the variety being contained within the following reports: C Fox's 'A Beaker barrow, enlarged in the Middle Bronze Age, at South Hill, Talbenny, Pembrokeshire' (*Archaeological Journal*, volume 99, 1942). C Fox's 'A Bronze Age barrow (Sutton 268') in Llandow parish, Glamorganshire' (*Archaeologia*, volume 89, 1943). W F Grimes's 'A Beaker-burial from Ludchurch, Pembrokeshire' (*Archaeologia Cambrensis*, volume 8, 1928). F M Lynch's 'A record of the Beaker cist found in 1937 at Llithfaen, Caernarfonshire' (*Archaeologia Cambrensis*, volume 134, 1985). H N Savory's 'A Beaker cist at Brymbo' (*Transactions of the Denbighshire Historical Society*, volume 8, 1959). Taking a broader perspective, F Petersen's 'Multiple burial in Neolithic and Bronze Age England' (*The Archaeological Journal*, volume 129, 1972) and A Gibson's article in Larsson and Parker Pearson's *From Stonehenge to the Baltic* (cited above) provide insights into the variety of burial practices current at this time, beyond that of individual burial.

2200–1500 BC. A perspective from the east (pp 81–82)

The contemporary writings of the eastern civilisations provide an interesting counterpoint to the purely archaeological evidence available in western Europe. Useful starters include A George's translation of *The epic of Gilgamesh* (Penguin Press, 1999) and M Lichtheim's *Ancient Egyptian literature* (University of California Press, 1975).

The quote by W O Stanley which begins this chapter is published in the *Archaeological Journal* (volume 7, 1850, pages 68-69). Work continues at the Great Orme, which is now open as a visitor attraction, with key sources worth consulting including C A Lewis's *Prehistoric mining at the Great Orme* the results of a Masters thesis, which is available from Great Orme Mines website. An overview of the above ground workings has been published as A Dutton and P J Fasham 'Prehistoric copper mining on the Great Orme, Llandudno, Gwynedd' (*Proceedings of the Prehistoric Society*, volume 60, 1994). S Oppenheimer's genetic study of people living around the Great Orme is available in summary form in *Origins of the British* (Robinson Publishing, 2007). References to other early mines have already been noted in the previous section.

Debate about the source of the copper used in the Castell Coch hoard can be found in S Needham's article in M Bartelheim, E Pernicka and R Krause's *The beginnings of metallurgy in the old world* (Rahden/Westf, 2002). What little information exists about the early exploitation of tin is summarised in R D Penhallurick's *Tin in antiquity* (Institute of Metals, 1986). Savory's *Guide catalogue* (cited above) remains a good overview of the development of metalwork styles in Wales, and examples of carvings of metal axes can be found in R J Bradley's *Rock art and the prehistory of Atlantic Europe* (Routledge, 1997).

F E S Roe has produced several useful articles which summarise the range of forms of the axe-hammer, see article in T H M Clough and W A Cummins's, *Stone axe studies* (Council for British Archaeology, 1979) and *The battle-axe series in Britain* (Proceedings of the Prehistoric Society, volume 32, 1966). The quote relating to the boy playing with an axe-hammer can be found in H N Jerman's 'Some unrecorded finds from east central Wales' (*Archaeologia Cambrensis*, volume 89, 1934). Work at the Hyssington production site has been published by N Jones and S Burrow in V Davis and M Edmonds's, *Stone axe studies, volume 3* (Oxbow Books, 2011). Discussion about the source of the 'bluestone' axe heads can be found in O Williams-Thorpe, M C Jones, P J Potts and P C Webb's 'Preseli dolerite bluestones' (*Oxford Journal of Archaeology*, volume 25:1, 2006).

British flint daggers have not been discussed in detail for some time, although their potential is well illustrated by H S Green, C H Houlder and L H Keeley's 'A flint dagger from Ffair Rhos, Ceredigion, Dyfed, Wales' (*Proceedings of the Prehistoric Society*, volume 48, 1982). Jet and jet-like materials in Wales have been reviewed by A Sheridan and M Davis's article in A Gibson and D Simpson's, *Prehistoric ritual and religion* (Sutton Publishing, 1998). Amber is reviewed in A Sheridan and A Shortland's article in I A G Shepherd and G J Barclay's, *Scotland in ancient Europe: the Neolithic and Early Bronze Age of Scotland in their European context* (Society of Antiquaries of Scotland, 2004). Eogan's *Accomplished art* (cited above), provides a good introduction to early goldwork, as does J J Taylor's *Bronze Age goldwork of the British Isles* (Cambridge University Press, 1980), a more recent appraisal of the evidence can be found in S Needham's 'The development of embossed goldwork in Bronze Age Europe' (*Antiquaries Journal*, volume 80, 2000).

2200–1500 BC. The dead in their thousands (pp 103–130)

Cadw's Wales-wide survey of burial sites from this period has been published in a number of county journals for example *Transactions of the Anglesey Antiquarian Society and Field Club* (2004), *Flintshire Historical Society Journal* (2003), and *The Montgomeryshire Collections* (2002).

For important reports on mountain top cairns see P Crew's 'The excavation of a group of mountain-top cairns on Drosgl, Llanllechid, Gwynedd' (*Bulletin of the Board of Celtic Studies*, volume 32, 1985) and A M Gibson's 'Survey, excavation and palaeoenvironmental investigations on Pen-y-fan and Corn-du, Brecon Beacons, Powys' (*Studia Celtica*, volume 31, 1997). While for the development of a burial landscape see F M Lynch's *Excavations in the Brenig Valley* (Cambrian Archaeological Association, 1993).

The key burial sites at Treiorwerth and Bedd Branwen are published in F M Lynch's 'Report on the re-excavation of two Bronze Age cairns in Anglesey' (*Archaeologia Cambrensis*, volume 120, 1971). Further radiocarbon dates from these sites have been published in A L Brindley's *The dating of food vessels and urns in Ireland* (National University of Ireland, 2007). The pioneering DNA studies at Bedd Branwen can be found in K A Brown, K O'Donoghue and T A Brown's 'DNA in cremated bones from an Early Bronze Age cemetery cairn' (*International Journal of Osteoarchaeology*, volume 5, 1995). Anglesey flat cemeteries are discussed in F M Lynch's *Prehistoric Anglesey* (Anglesey Antiquarian Society, 1991).

Turning to cremation rites, the quote from *Gilgamesh* on page 115 is from A George's translation cited above, and a flavour of J McKinley's work on cremated remains from this period can be found in 'Bronze Age 'barrows' and funerary rites and rituals of cremation' (*Proceedings of the Prehistoric Society*, volume 63, 1997). The variation in the size of Welsh cremation deposits is described in F M Lynch's 'Moel Goedog Circle I, a complex ring cairn near Harlech' (*Archaeologia Cambrensis*, volume 133, 1984). The quote on page 126 is derived from W O Stanley's 'Account of sepulchral deposit, with cinerary urns, found at Porth Dafarch, in Holyhead Island' (*Archaeological Journal*, volume 6, 1849).

In addition to the references listed above, a good overview of the burial rites from this period is available in A Woodward's *British Barrows* (Tempus, 2000). For an introduction to burial urns see I H Longworth's *Collared urns of the Bronze Age in Great Britain and Ireland* (Cambridge University Press, 1984). For their provenance in Wales see J Ll Williams and D A Jenkins's 'Petrographic analysis and classification of prehistoric pottery from northern Wales' (*Studia Celtica*, volume 38, 2004).

2200–1500 BC. What the dead took with them (pp 131–151)

Savory's *Guide catalogue* (cited above) is a key resource for this chapter, although many discoveries have been made subsequent to its publication. For a broader introduction to the range of grave goods found across Britain see D V Clarke, T G Cowie and A Foxon's *Symbols of power at the time of Stonehenge* (Stationery Office, 1985).

Many publications detailing discoveries at key burial sites for this period have already been referenced above; but a number of additional sources can be recommended which take a broader perspective on specific themes raised in this chapter. The intriguing subject of personal grooming towards the end of this time is explored in R M Kavanagh's 'A reconsideration of razors in the Irish Earlier Bronze Age' (*Journal of the Royal Society of Antiquaries of Ireland*, volume 121, 1991). The apparent 'arms race' at this time is discussed in A Harding's article in J Carman and A Harding's *Ancient warfare* (Sutton Publishing, 1999), with a broader view of the subject appearing in J Guilaine and J Zammit's *The origins of war* (Blackwell publishing, 2001). Discussion about the function of wristguards can be found in A Woodward, J Hunter, R Ixer, F Roe, P J Potts, P C Webb, J S Watson and M C Jones's 'Beaker age bracers in England' (*Antiquity*, volume 80, 2006). And analytical study of 'pygmy cups' and the nature of these miniature vessels is published in A Gibson and B Stern's article in A Gibson's, *Prehistoric pottery* (British Archaeological Reports, 2006).

2200–1500 BC. Before they died (pp 152–172)

The scarcity of houses from this period has long been noted; the two best preserved ones in Wales are published in D Benson, J G Evans, G H Williams, T C Darvill and A E U David's 'Excavations at Stackpole Warren, Dyfed' (*Proceedings of the Prehistoric Society*, volume 56, 1990) and A E Caseldine, G Smith and C J Griffiths's 'Vegetation history and upland settlement at Llyn Morwynion, Ffestiniog, Meirionnydd' (*Archaeology in Wales*, volume 41, 2001). More information about the possible house / burial skeumorph at Aber Camddwr can be found in E C Marshall and K Murphy's 'The excavation of two Bronze Age cairns with associated standing stones in Dyfed: Parc Maen and Aber Camddwr II' (*Archaeologia Cambrensis*, volume 140, 1991).

Discussion about the role of burnt mounds continues with a good introduction to the subject being available in V Buckley's *Burnt offerings* (Wordwell, 1990). For attempts to replicate the use of these sites see M J O'Kelly's 'Excavations and experiments in ancient Irish cooking-places' (*Journal of the Royal Society of Antiquaries of Ireland*, volume 84:2, 1954) and H J James's 'Excavations of burnt mounds at Carne, nr Fishguard' (*Bulletin of the Board of Celtic Studies*, volume 33, 1986).

Introductions to the major 'ceremonial' sites from this period include A Burl's *The stone circles of Britain, Ireland and Brittany* (Yale University Press, 2000) which includes the quote given on page 166, A Gibson's *Stonehenge and timber circles* (Tempus, 1998) and A H Ward's 'Survey and excavation of ring cairns in SE Dyfed and on Gower, West Glamorgan' (*Proceedings of the Prehistoric Society*, volume 54, 1988). To this can be added F Pryor's *Seahenge* (HarperCollins, 2002) which provides much food for thought, if not many answers, about the types of activities which may have occurred within these sites. The astronomical significance of stone circles remains a fascination for many, drawing in particular on work by Alexander Thom, for a considered discussion of this subject see C Ruggles's *Astronomy in prehistoric Britain and Ireland* (Yale University Press, 1999).

V Cummings and R Johnston's *Prehistoric journeys* (Oxbow Books, 2007) provides an introduction to this difficult subject, with an important article by Roberts on the landscape around Penmaenmawr being of particular relevance. The possible routeways in Merionethshire are considered in E G Bowen and C A Gresham's *History of Merioneth, volume 1* (The Merioneth Historical and Record Society, 1967), and those in the Welsh borders in L F Chitty's article in I L Foster and L Alcock's, *Culture and environment* (Routledge & Kegan Paul, 1963). For those attempting to fit Wales's story alongside that of the West Midlands, P Garwood's *The undiscovered country* (Oxbow Books, 2007) is recommended. Finally, the story of what happened in Wales next can be picked up in the later chapters of F M Lynch, S Aldhouse-Green and J L Davies's *Prehistoric Wales* (Sutton, 2000) and C J Arnold and J L Davies's *Roman & Early Medieval Wales* (Sutton, 2000).

Index